Game Changer

Celebrating
30 Years of Publishing
in India

Praise for Shahid Afridi

'Shahid Afridi's competitiveness, his never-say-die attitude, his spirit, his energy: all so impressive. A great servant to cricket and to his country.'
—**Sir Vivian Richards**

'As brave as a warrior … Shahid Afridi is one of the strongest men I've known.'—**Wasim Akram**

'When runs were needed, and the big shots were required, and when his bat was responding, Shahid Afridi could be the most dangerous player.'
—**Sachin Tendulkar**

'In modern cricket, the only man who can evacuate a stadium by walking off the pitch is Afridi.'—**Ramiz Raja**

'A born entertainer. To have played all three forms for such a long career, with the pressure he has to deal with, and under the weight of expectations that he has to deliver every time, that's something special.'
—**Kevin Pietersen**

'Of Shahid Afridi it can safely be said that cricket never has and never will see another like him. To say he is an all-rounder is to say Albert Einstein was a scientist; it tells a criminally bare story.'
—**Osman Samiuddin**, journalist, author, *The Unquiet Ones: The History of Pakistan Cricket*

'What makes Shahid Afridi popular? What makes Afridi popular is what makes a eunuch's bawdy joke popular; it's what makes slapstick popular; it's what makes us enjoy the cheap and the risqué. Whatever makes Afridi popular is an impulse – a primordial, preprogrammed reaction – that people with expensive educations are embarrassed about experiencing. What makes Afridi popular is not something you'll ever have to teach your children, though you'll probably be tempted to teach them to forget it. What makes Afridi popular is as vast as the sky, and just as obvious.'—**Ahmer Naqvi**, journalist

Game Changer

Shahid Afridi

WITH **WAJAHAT S. KHAN**

FOREWORD BY WASIM AKRAM

Harper
Sport

First published in hardback in India in 2019 by Harper Sport
An imprint of HarperCollins *Publishers*
4th Floor, Tower A, Building No. 10, DLF Cyber City,
DLF Phase II, Gurugram, Haryana – 122002
www.harpercollins.co.in

This edition published in India by Harper Sport 2023

2 4 6 8 10 9 7 5 3 1

Front cover and poster photograph copyright
© Amean J | 18% Grey

P-ISBN: 978-93-5699-596-3
E-ISBN: 978-93-5302-672-1

Typeset in 11/14.7 Minion Pro at
Manipal Digital Systems, Manipal

Printed and bound at
Replika Press Pvt. Ltd.

To the women who have made us.
To the men who have led us.
To the enemies who have hardened us.
To the friends who have trusted us.
And to the game changers who will follow us.

CONTENTS

FOREWORD

LIKE ALL great discoveries, it started with a need. We were in a tri-series in Kenya in 1996. Mushtaq Ahmed, our dependable World Cup champion leg spinner, was injured. So here we were, stuck in Africa, in dire need of a leggie, and in comes this kid, kind of chubby but straight-edged and quiet. None of us had heard of him before.

The selectors had picked him with some sense of hope. They said he was all right. We were like, 'Okay, sure ... why not? He might work out.' But at the time, he was an unknown resource. Almost unnoticeable.

When he arrived in Nairobi and began bowling in the nets, I remember he came at us hard and fast. He had variety. He was a teenager, very agile. I remember he had a solid googly, a good faster one, and could change it up quite effortlessly. Instinctively, his bowling was less Mushtaq Ahmed and more Anil Kumble. Could have been taller, I remember telling myself.

Then came the time for him to bat. It was beginning to get dark. There wasn't much light left. He was the only one who hadn't batted. We were in a hurry to get back to the hotel. It wouldn't have been a

major loss – bowlers never got to bat much in the nets in those days.
What the hell, I thought, and asked him to pad up.

What happened next didn't let us make it to the hotel in time.
First, I started bowling him leg-breaks. I was firmly dispatched. Next,
Waqar (Younis) started bowling off-breaks to him. His deliveries too
were smacked, viciously. Then, both Waqar and I tried bowling at
him with a short run-up. Both of us were sent packing.

I was still sceptical. Clearly this was a *tuqqa*, a lucky strike. So
we took longer run-ups and came hard at him. The kid just kept
hitting us all over. The harder we came at him, the more confidently
he struck the ball. Not once did he seem to flinch. Nor did he
break into a sweat. He hit us for sixes in the dark, like he had night
vision or something. Soon I decided to call it off. This was getting
embarrassing.

The next day I told him to pad up early. This time, right from
ball one, Waqar and I came at him with a full run-up. But the kid
was relentless. He hit us harder than he had the previous evening. I
remember thinking that the sort of shots he was hammering, had it
not been for the nets, the ball would have gone out of the stadium.

It was on that day in the nets that it became clear to me: there was
talent. This boy had the potential to go places.

But then news came in of my father having suffered a heart attack.
As I was packing to fly back to Lahore, I suggested to Saeed Anwar,
who was to captain in my absence, to let the kid bat up the order.

It was just a suggestion. Saeed knew what he was doing. I didn't
know that a casual suggestion would make history. Back in Lahore,
I heard the news before I actually saw that famous match against
Sri Lanka. I read about it in the papers the morning after. That
afternoon, I actually saw the damn innings.

It was the stuff of legend: a quick-fire 37-ball century for the ages.
That too in 1996, a time when even 230 was considered a defendable
total.

Later that night, I saw the innings again. I knew Shahid Afridi was here to stay.

But let's be honest. I didn't discover Afridi. He would have made it anyway. Although I knew that he had what we Lahoris call *pharak*, the spark. That's why I took him under my wing.

Afridi was a shy boy when he started. He wasn't the abrasive, tough guy you see today. He was like any average teenager, a bit awkward. It's not difficult to imagine why. Think about it. The Pakistan line-up he was exposed to at the beginning – Waqar Younis, Saleem Malik, Ramiz Raja, Ijaz Ahmed, Saeed Anwar ... He probably had our posters in his room. And then, just like that, he was among us. It would have been a difficult transition for anyone.

I soon realized that he needed a confidence boost. So I took him on as a project. I started taking him with me to meet folks. I began polishing him, making him come along to dinners and events. I've always believed that if you're a confident person yourself, it starts showing in your line of work too. Shahid Afridi, the teenager, needed that affirmation.

I captained him for 10 years or so, on and off. We became very fond of each other, of course. But I do wonder if we made him perform what we had hired him for: a quick-fire leggie in the team. I know that he has regrets about how his skill sets were not utilized properly.

But here's the reality. In Pakistan cricket, we don't do the whole personal psyche thing. We don't think about what the other person is thinking. We are not proactive. Imran Khan was. But he was Imran Khan. There's never been – and there may never be – anyone like him.

Unfortunately, by the time Afridi dug his roots in the Pakistan side, a crisis of confidence had developed not only in the team but also in my captaincy, a role that was assigned to me sporadically. He should have had more confident people around him to shape and chisel and hone him. But he did not. He was unlucky that way. Also, he was so young. He got too much attention. There was too much happening, too soon, for him.

Some of us stood up for him. I remember having an argument with the selectors prior to the 1999 tour of India. I wanted him in the squad, the selectors did not. Eventually, I put my foot down – I knew he was a match winner – and said that I would rather resign from the post of captain if Afridi didn't make it to the Test squad. The selectors finally gave in. Afridi proved himself: in the first Test, he smashed 141. He badgered the hell out of India. He became a sensation all over again. I stood redeemed.

But had Afridi known about his own talent, he could have been so much more. He was constantly missing the confidence to settle down. He needed someone to tell him, 'Pathan, you have so much already. Now fix your technique and see the places you can go.' That's what was missing.

To become great, you need self-confidence. He had what it took for any World XI to have his name. I don't like comparing the eras, but the 1990s were very difficult for a player like Afridi. It was tough to open the way he did, to hit like he did. Every opponent team had three pacers who could top speeds of 150 km/hr. It wasn't a walk in the park to have the sort of strike rate he introduced to the game.

But his reflexes, his hand–eye coordination, his natural flair and aggression – it was unbelievable. It was also very frustrating for us, the way he could move, just pick the ball and scoop it – either out of the park or right into the hands of mid-on. Yes, he struggled in the Test era, but once the age of T20s began, there was no looking back. It was a format tailormade for him.

Afridi wasn't limited by any means. But he limited himself. At the international level, if you believe that you don't have what it takes, then you will not produce what is required of you. You need to believe in yourself. You have to set boundaries: 'I will leave the short ball, I will defend outside off stump.' You must follow the basic rules. Afridi, it was proved over time, is just human.

I didn't approve of his starts and stops. For example, the way he quit captaincy in 2010 after leading Pakistan in just one Test. It showed that he hadn't thought the plan through. Today, if you want to be a known quantity, you must be someone who's in it for the long-term.

But no matter what Afridi has achieved and despite his retirement from the Pakistan side, stadiums fill up for him even today when he plays limited-overs formats. He is an impact player. A cricketer for any era. He is a star. I wasn't sure about his charisma in the early days, though. By 1999, I realized it was there. The aura around him was building.

I remember a match against Zimbabwe. We had a packed stadium in Peshawar. Absolutely chock-a-block. There were more people outside the stadium than there were inside. The crowd was going nuts, screaming his name. He came in, pulled a high one, it came off his glove and he was caught, first ball. The crowd went nuts and attempted to break the gates – they wanted him to have another go. They said it was a 'try ball', like it was a street match. The cops had to come in with water cannons and tear gas. It's remarkable that Afridi had that star power just a couple of years into the Pakistan team.

The crucial thing about Afridi is that everything he does and doesn't do works. Sure, he's got an image. He's a fit guy. He's got the looks. And I'm so proud of the work he's done for the Shahid Afridi Foundation.

But you don't just become a star. You must be aware of what's going on around you too. I tried to learn. I still do. You live it up, sure, but you have to know your stuff too.

Was he easy to lead? Yes. Was he there when the team needed him? Yes. Was he up for taking the pressure? Yes. Up for any tough fielding position? Always. No hesitation. Not even for a moment. Afridi was as brave as a warrior. He is one of the strongest men I've known. It's been said that he has a problem with authority. Fine, but only with authority which is not worth respecting. You have to know his psyche to lead him. He is not stubborn at all. You must know what you're dealing with. If he respects you, he will put his life on the firing line for you.

Sure, it was a treat to have him, and I enjoyed leading him. I took it as a challenge. Saqlain Mushtaq, Abdul Razzaq, Azhar Mahmood, Shoaib Akhtar, Shahid Afridi – when all of them were in the same playing eleven, especially in the shorter format, it made the Pakistan team invincible.

But as a captain, nobody kept me on edge more than Afridi did. One couldn't even go to the loo when he was playing in the middle. That's because he could change any game, any time. He was and will remain a game changer.

Wasim Akram

PREFACE

BOTH OF us were in our teens.

He was on a lush ground in Nairobi, running his gloves through the hair flopping over his eyes, glancing over his shoulder like someone had thrown a rock at him from the stands behind square leg. This would become his habit over the years: his nervous, over-the-shoulder twitch, as if an enemy sniper was lurking in the stands.

I was at economics tuition, in a dingy Karachi high-rise.

He started.

I stopped studying – we all did – as that 37-ball century we had heard about unfolded on the TV screen.

They weren't showing the match live. But it didn't matter.

In those 37 balls, a new era of the game cleaved. A new approach birthed.

From a snowy, static-lined TV, he formed a collective memory for all of us in that room. In so many rooms.

Nerds and jocks, babes and bums, all economists about to graduate from private school, all college-bound, all hoping for early success, saw it happen in real time to a middle-class kid from 'across the bridge' in Karachi.

One of the girls said he was cute. One of the jocks noted that he wasn't classy. They didn't matter. Nobody was listening.

In those 37 balls, an imperfect hero, a street-hustling Pathan from the wrong side of the tracks, recreated stardom in the gentleman's game.

The glue was his disrespect for tradition.

His lonesomeness was his weapon. He would hone it.

There was no *sajda* when he hit 100. No humble prostration before the Almighty by kissing the ground. No worship or thanks. There was no bat raise, no helmet in the air.

There wasn't even any acknowledgement of the dressing room, where his teammates were on their feet.

There was a jerk, his blade reloaded like a shotgun, and a march back to the crease that almost took out the stumps as he went back to work.

The Butcher. The Beast. The Boy Wonder. The Boom Boom.

Our game, his way. That's what he played.

And we would let him have his way.

Over hundreds of transmissions, I would see him fly, soar, crash and burn.

And then we would meet, exactly twenty years later, on another hot afternoon, in another battleground: his birthplace, the mountains of Khyber Pass.

He would size me up. We would make a pact.

And then this happened.

This book is for all the game changers.

And for Muma, Baba, Fatima and Daddy.

And for Arya, Sasha and Simin.

And, of course, for Shaan.

– Wajahat S. Khan, Karachi, 2019

INTRODUCTION

THIS IS the first autobiography of Shahid Afridi, one of cricket's most controversial and popular all-rounders and Pakistan's biggest cricketing superstar since Imran Khan.

Afridi's story must be told. His is a tale that begins with the cricket world's most famous batting debut when, at age nineteen, not sixteen as has been believed till now, he scored a 37-ball century – the fastest the world had ever seen – against then world champions Sri Lanka. Since that incredible innings in Nairobi on 4 October 1996, Afridi's career has been quite similar to that of a suddenly successful Hollywood star who stumbles in and out of scandal, is led astray by his youth, good looks, talent and overconfidence, but is still adored for his performances.

Yet, over twenty years since his swashbuckling start, it is clear that Afridi is not a one-hit wonder. Despite inconsistent performances, he is one of the few cricketers to have earned a globally recognized nickname – Boom Boom – for his aggressive, take-no-prisoners batting that has disappointed his fans as often as it has ripped through his opponents' bowling attacks. Along the way, he has landed championships, dug pitches, tampered balls, played politics, broken sledging rules and won hearts – all while reinventing himself mid-career as a brutally aggressive and freakishly quick leg-spinner who gets sponsors as quickly as he collects scalps. Today, Afridi is considered an unpredictable bad boy of the gentleman's game. But in a sport dented by corruption, he is still an honourable man.

Game Changer is the story of one of modern cricket's most controversial and high-achieving practitioners. Charted over the course of Afridi's life, from the mountains of Pakistan's unruly northwest to the mean streets of Karachi to the county grounds of southern England, this is a modern, personalized history of a global cricket legend, told as a memoir. It captures the journey of his unconventional rise, his overnight – and controversial – stardom, his weaknesses, greatest moments on the field and his future ambitions, political or otherwise. Moreover, his story is also a tale of the violent, corrupt and terror-prone Pakistan that Afridi has played in and for, and is told by one of her greatest sons.

'Of Shahid Afridi it can safely be said that cricket never has and never will see another like him,' wrote Osman Samiuddin, author of *The Unquiet Ones: A History of Pakistan Cricket* and one of the most distinct observers of cricket in South Asia, back in the mid-2000s. 'To say he is an all-rounder is to say Albert Einstein was a scientist; it tells a criminally bare story.'[1]

This book, therefore, attempts to unravel the many sides of Afridi for his fans. For the commoner on the streets of Pakistan, he is a modern Islamic demi-god, complete with his resplendent beard and open religiosity. In a London pub quiz, he is a cricket statistician's outlier, defying odds, traditions and averages. On an Australian beach, he embodies the ribald, defiant desperation of the colonized, an angry and hungry adversary who feasted on a cricket ball as millions Down Under watched him fail miserably at cheating a game away from their squad of dispassionate, well-paid professionals. And in an Indian living room, he is 'the other', the flamboyant, talented,

---

[1] http://www.espncricinfo.com/pakistan/content/player/42639.html

in-your-face belligerent Pashtun warrior, the one Pakistani who has been frequently fined, often beaten but never vanquished, on or off the field.

But on a pitch, anywhere in the world of cricket, Afridi is anathema to the orthodox, and ecstasy for the game changers. Thus the title of this book – about all these aspects of Afridi and more. Surely, the most predictable thing about Afridi today is his unpredictability.

Obviously, the magnitude of his achievements is featured, even questioned. Despite the inconsistency and the immaturity, his compulsive, shameless hitting has led to records that are staggering. Besides a quick-fire first century, Afridi claimed the prize of scoring the second-fastest half-century the game has ever seen. Also, as ESPNcricinfo analyses, Afridi hit more sixes (476) in international cricket than any other man who has ever played the game, a record that stood for nearly a decade until West Indies opener Chris Gayle broke it in February 2019.[2]

When that shocking statistic is coupled with the highest strike rate among players who have batted in at least 50 innings, and further compounded by his appearing thrice in the top seven list of the fastest one day international (ODI) hundreds, five times in the top twelve list of fastest ODI fifties, even as he rules the eighth house of the all-time list of most ODI wickets *while* having the highest strike rate ever in an international innings, and being casually ranked by *The Wisden Cricketer* as the 'third most feared batsman'[3] by international bowlers, he becomes something else – a nuclear-powered, tactically gone rogue, highly potent and very misunderstood sportsman, similar to the perception about Pakistan, as a nation, in the world today.

---

[2] http://stats.espncricinfo.com/icc-odi/content/records/284025.html.

[3] Cricinfo Staff, 'Gilchrist voted scariest batsman', ESPNcricinfo, July 17, 2005, http://www.espncricinfo.com/australia/content/story/211318.html.

In the following pages, Afridi's complex life and multifaceted career are mapped through a personal journey with the man himself. He has lots of colourful anecdotes to share about his humble beginnings in the warring tribal areas in northwest Pakistan, from where he emigrated to the rough alleys of Karachi in the 1980s. His schooldays, mostly spent bunking classes and playing cricket, are not disconnected from the rise of organized violence in Pakistan's dangerous megacity, where he admits to hanging out with thugs after late-night street cricket matches.

A working-class hero who isn't from the 'Oxbridge' vintage of former Pakistani greats, Afridi's tale also features his confrontation with poverty in an increasingly struggling and corrupt Pakistan, while being the fifth of eleven siblings in a lower middle-class household. Prominently featured is his role in Pakistan's 2010 match-fixing scandal and how he survived it, while calling others out, only to come back stronger. As *The Cricket Monthly* assesses, at home he 'is revered not for his achievements but for his promise. Afridi is the last folk hero, a man loved by his people because he doesn't live how they should but rather how they do'.[4]

Game Changer is not a conventional autobiography – one which only describes his early years, his rise to fame, his laurels and falls, his big matches and so on – but an imaginative, personal history that befits a globally known sports star from a 'war on terror' zone. Thus, another relevant theme touched, perhaps popularly orientalist in nature, is his innate Pashtun tribalism, not a culture that even the two-century-old, colonially gentrified game was familiar with before he arrived on the scene.

As ESPNcricinfo notes, the phenomenon of Afridi 'has to do with his DNA':

4 Ahmer Naqvi, 'Starman, countryman', The Cricket Monthly, February 2015, http://www.thecricketmonthly.com/story/825081/starman--countryman.

The Afridi tribe originated from brutal mountainous terrain overlapping Afghanistan and Pakistan. Even today, the name evokes ferocity, daring and fearlessness. Shahid Afridi's approach to cricket has been nothing short of tribal warfare. Background, context and meaning are pushed to the periphery. It's all about the immediacy of the challenge, the moment of conflict, the act of confrontation and battle.[5]

These premises and sub-narratives attempt to meet the expectations for a cutting-edge, tell-all, no-nonsense autobiography of a controversial man from a controversial country. Self-documented and introspective, featuring never-before-seen photographs from his personal collection, this book is a testimony from a modern athlete about things local, global and conflicted, besides the usual trappings of what makes him a modern athlete. As the *Wisden Cricketer* declares, Afridi stands out in a game of blending in, as he is 'in everyone's face: mildly threatening, breaking through, scoring crucial runs, turning games, playing games within games, cheerleading and celebrating, right in the thick of it.'[6]

---

[5] Saad Shafqat, 'The leggie trapped in a slogger's identity', ESPNcricinfo, June 11, 2012, http://www.espncricinfo.com/magazine/content/story/567955.html.

[6] Osman Samiuddin, 'Mad, bad and dangerous', ESPNcricinfo, June 2005, http://www.espncricinfo.com/wac/content/story/224694.html.

If you wanna flash, flash hard
If you wanna touch the stars,
If you wanna flash, flash hard

Everybody say, 'Boom Boom, Afridi'

If you wanna hear the crowd
Screaming out your name, so loud
If you wanna hear the crowd

Say 'Boom Boom, Afridi'
Everybody say, 'Boom Boom, Afridi'

—The Duckworth-Lewis Method

1

TAKING A STANCE

MY NAME is Sahibzada Mohammad Shahid Khan Afridi. It's a long name and I'm proud of it.

The records say I was born on 1 March. That makes me a Piscean, although I think I am Sagittarian. But I don't believe much in such things, so I wouldn't know. No reason, really. I don't believe I know the future. Unlike many others, I don't like predicting my own future either. I like taking things one ball at a time.

I don't have many memories of my international debut in Nairobi in 1996, where I smashed that century for the record books in just my second ODI, the fastest the world had seen. But I remember being young, weightless and peerless as one feels at that age. I remember being carefree as I stepped on to the field with the very men I had revered as a kid, the cricket gods of that era. I also remember not being able to sleep much the night before that match. I remember a dream where I was hitting the big shots against the best in the world. And then I remember crowds rejoicing. Everywhere.

It is said that I 'changed the game' after that century but, honestly, the game changed me as well. In the public eye, I became someone else – not necessarily someone I had wanted to become.

I may have changed the game and let the game change me, but everything remained the same at home. I have six brothers and five sisters. I'm number five in the 11-member cricket team that is my family. I was four or five when I played cricket for the first time. I can't remember which habit I picked up first, bowling or batting. But I remember playing hard and fast.

My name is Shahid Afridi. I've represented the Pakistan cricket team for over twenty years in some of the toughest times in my great country's history. I've broken records, bats and hearts in the greatest game ever played. It might hurt some and it might not be what everyone would want to read, but here in these pages is my story. I only wish my father and mother – whom I dedicate these words to – were alive to read it.

2
IN THE BEGINNING, JUST WAR AND CRICKET

BY THE time I started walking, sometime in the early 1980s, Pakistan was crazy about just three sports: cricket, hockey and squash. Cricket was the most popular of them, and more accessible, as it could be played on the streets. It was more appealing too because there were a lot of stars at the time in the Pakistan team who inspired young men, even women, to play the sport.

Like millions of others in my generation, my star was Imran Khan. I started playing cricket because of him. Like him, I fancied myself as a fast bowler, though unlike many, I never tried to mimic his action. However, when I realized that my bowling action was problematic – I'd chuck the ball when I bowled pace – I quit fast bowling.

Like any other middle-class kid in Pakistan, I started playing in the neighbourhood, on the streets. The area I lived in, the roughshod Federal 'B' Area of Karachi, Pakistan's former capital and now its most troubled megacity with over 20 million people, wasn't as violent in the '80s as it is today and a lot of first-class cricketers lived there at the time.

I remember that my vicinity, Block 10, a warm neighbourhood where everyone knew each other, had a lot of cricketers. Haroon Rasheed, who played several Tests in the '70s for Pakistan and is credited for discovering Waqar Younis, was my neighbour and an inspiration. So was my elder brother, Tariq, who played first-class cricket and was a very quick pace bowler during his playing days.

Like many middle-class South Asian parents, my father, Sahibzada Fazal Rehman Afridi – God bless his soul – was not very happy about my interest in cricket. My family had traditionally always been in business or the armed forces. The ups and downs and unpredictability of cricket didn't fit into my father's world of trying to make a stable, honest living, as is the Pashtun way. He would be livid when I would come back home after hours and give me plenty of flak for wasting my day, for letting the outdoors darken my complexion and for not hitting the books hard enough at school. I think he wanted me to become a doctor or something, because on particularly angry days, he used to warn: 'Even if you don't have the capacity to walk, even if your back fails you, you can still sit on a chair at a desk and prescribe medicine.' Clearly, he wasn't a believer in my passion for cricket. Not in those early days.

My father had his reasons to be sceptical about a career in cricket. I was born in Tirah, Maidan, a valley in the mountains of Khyber. It is a remote area in the northwest region of Pakistan and home to my fellow Afridi tribesmen. Traditionally, the Afridis, who are divided into several sub-tribes, have enjoyed the reputation of fighting everyone, be it the Mughals or the British. We have defended the famous Khyber Pass for hundreds of years and have a can-do-anything reputation when it comes to protecting our land.

The Afridi tribe lives on both sides of the Pakistan–Afghanistan border, an area that has witnessed a lot of fighting and terrorist activities in recent decades. When my immediate family was living there, terrorism wasn't rampant. But fights and feuds were common and that made them move to Tangibanda in Kohat, another hub of

Afridi tribesmen. Kohat is also a part of the unruly northwest, but it's located more towards the mainland and is therefore less volatile as a region.

Migrating was easy. It's in our blood. All Pashtuns take pride in being warring tribesmen. But we also have a very strong work ethic and always go where work requires us to. It's true: we Pashtuns love to work. We are up for any sort of labour. In Pakistan, Pashtuns dominate the construction and transportation industries, and also make up a good chunk of the army. Our hardiness is an asset that has made us the finest bricklayers and the toughest soldiers. That's why it is said that when a Pashtun isn't working, he's fighting.

In the precarious '80s, as the global superpowers faced off in Afghanistan and Pakistan's tribal areas became the frontline for what would become the longest war of our time, there wasn't much work in Kohat. In search of a living, my father shifted to Karachi, Pakistan's largest city and the 'promised land' for many Pashtuns because of its free, entrepreneurial spirit. Once he was fairly settled in Karachi, he brought the rest of us there.

My father started off humbly in the city. Karachi has always had a water-shortage problem and he joined the water-tanker business, supplying water to those who could afford it. Along the way he received some help from cousins and friends, as is the Pashtun way of networking within the family. A couple of years later, he got into car sales and started dealing in used and new cars. He set up what they call in Karachi a 'showroom', and in Peshawar a 'bargain'. Despite their hardiness, trade comes easily to Pashtuns, especially Afridis. My father kept on expanding the business and even invested in a bunch of small ventures here and there. By the end of a decade in Karachi, we weren't doing too badly for a middle-class family in a middle-class neighbourhood.

And then rushed in the military. My paternal uncle, Colonel Akram Afridi, was a decorated infantry officer of the 19th Baloch Regiment. As my father never had the time for sports, 'Kaka' Akram must be credited for introducing sports to our family. He had seen the world outside Tirah and Kohat, having been posted all over Pakistan. In the army, he had played some cricket and volleyball, the latter being a typically army sport – soldiers would set up a net anywhere and play. When he would come back on vacation to our village, he played cricket with my other uncles and relatives. Cricket was like a gift he brought with him every time he visited. That's how I picked up the game, in the mountains of northwest Pakistan, thanks to an exposed, well-travelled, soldiering uncle. That's where the influence came from – not from my father. No, definitely not from my father.

Honestly, my father wasn't so much against cricket as a sport. He was angry with me for hoping to play cricket as a profession, making it a long-term career – not as some sort of pastime. I remember the scolding and beatings I got from him because of my obsession with the game.

I guess it's understandable. I mean, him working hard and sending us to school, and me bunking school – private school, that too – and playing cricket wasn't exactly a good deal for him. To be honest, I'm pretty sure I deserved the beatings, at least from his perspective. But that didn't mean that I gave up the sport. Pathans are like water. The more you push us, the bigger the splash we make.

In Federal 'B' Area, my local club was Shadab Sports. At the time, Shadab was one of Karachi's finest. It housed some of the best first-class cricketers in a city that's at par with Lahore in producing the finest cricketing talent for Pakistan. Unlike today, back in the day, even the stars of first-class and club cricket commanded respect. And those guys got appreciation too.

I'm not exaggerating when I say that at the time, the value of a first-class cricketer was more than that of any international Pakistan player. In the neighbourhoods and clubs, people knew first-class players by name. They had street cred and were local legends. People would line up to see them play in their neighbourhoods, even if for a casual game. They were the gods of the homegrown cricket circuit.

At Shadab, Haroon Rasheed and his brother, Mohtashim Rasheed – who eventually became the national women's team's coach – would watch me in action.

Although a melting pot for cricket lovers in the neighbourhood, Shadab Sports wasn't much of a club when it came to facilities. Before the matches, we had to turn up with a broom and clean the pitch ourselves. Then around 2 p.m. we would start the nets.

They say there are two types of climate in Karachi: hot and very hot. For me, though, it was all the same. I remember it always being hot. Perhaps because I was a fast bowler in those days, I remember really feeling the heat. During the peak of summer, and especially during Ramadan, the matches would be moved to the night shift. Streets would become cricketing bazaars. Electricians would be hired to set up and take off the naked T-bulbs, set up via illegal 'kunda' connections to light up roads, alleys, even empty plots and garbage dumps. They say that in Karachi's blazing summers, only cricketers and thugs stay up at night.

Despite my chucking, or *wutta* – meaning 'throwing a stone' – as they call it in Pakistan, I continued with pace bowling. No coach or senior ever bothered fixing my bowling action. Pakistan's cricket clubs aren't exactly known for their coaching acumen – the talent of the players possibly makes up for it. I remember what brought an end to my pace bowling stint. One day, in the nets, a ball I bowled hit a batsman younger to me in the chest. He was almost knocked out and was barely breathing. That's when Mohtashim Rasheed, who was watching us, came to me and told me to stop *wutta* pace and try some proper spin, otherwise the kid would get hurt again. I didn't take his suggestion personally and just followed his advice. I was young, around twelve or thirteen years old, and needed the directive. I apologized to the kid and chose a shorter run-up.

I don't know why but in my next delivery, I ran in to bowl in the style and run-up of Abdul Qadir, a popular Pakistani leg-spinner from that era whom I used to watch on TV. Qadir would famously dance up to the crease, left and right and up and down, a waltz of confusion and strategy. As if on cue, I imitated him and threw one in. It was a pretty good ball: quick and a fast turner. The kid, already scared, couldn't do much with it. That's when Mohtashim Rasheed turned around and said, 'From today, you're only going to bowl spin. This fast-cum-spin thing you're doing is your style now. But fix your stupid dance. And remember: mix it up.'

From that day onwards, I continued bowling that way. At the U-14 level, I was selected as a bowler. But the batting bug remained in me. I could deliver with the blade from time to time – some of it had to do with my strength. I remember in a club game, I once went out to bat at No. 7 and slammed a century. I even took three wickets in that match. It was a proper cricket ground, quite large, and I hit a lot of sixes in that match. Professor Siraj-ul-Islam Bukhari, a legend in the Karachi City Cricket Association, was watching that game. He later called me over and asked, 'Those were some big sixes. Are you really a U-14 player?' By then, I had got used to the question and replied, 'Sir, all Pashtuns are strong. You need to make a ball of stone, not cork, if you want me to hit smaller sixes!'

3
SCHOOL CRICKET, MINUS
THE SCHOOL

IF YOU'RE a young boy or girl and reading this, here's some advice: do not drop out of school. That was my story but it doesn't necessarily have to be yours.

I never enjoyed school. Period. Except for the cricket. I could never hit the books or obsess about studying. I never really wanted to get on the doctor-lawyer-engineer gravy train. The only thing I ever obsessed about was cricket.

It was a handicap, I think. I should have studied harder. My father surely wanted me to. But I wonder, had I been more academically inclined, had I devoted more time towards studies and less towards playing the game, would I still have been the cricketer I became? To be honest, the best memories I have of school are all cricket-related. Maybe I've suppressed the memories of exams, classes and studying. My grades were pretty traumatizing.

My school attendance records read like I was a refugee or something – except that all of my schooling was in Karachi's tough central and north areas. First, I was at Al Munawara Academy in Federal 'B' Area, then at Bright Fox, Federal Secondary School and finally at Ibrahim Alibhai. Lots of moves. Lots of change. Lots of neighbourhoods. On purely academic terms, I found it tough to continue in private schools, so I had to settle for a public school. My father was not in favour of this decision but my brother, Tariq, prompted him to admit me into a government school. After all, my family members had, more or less, given up on my academic performance. At least the quality of cricket was better at public schools, Tariq reasoned.

Public school was a good gig for me. I fit in. All the private-school outcasts were in that system. It was an aggressive, dog-eat-dog environment. Alphas only. Omegas were not welcome and usually got chewed up like bones. And the cricket – it was fantastic, bare-knuckle stuff.

Still, I regret not studying more; less for myself than for my father. He was a Pashtun, not so well educated himself. He was conservative and ambitious and really wanted me to get a decent education. Naturally, he did not approve of my full-time obsession with cricket, a game he believed would leave me with no other options. (In hindsight, he was right.) But at the time, I took his warning as a challenge. I'd already disappointed him in studies. Failure in cricket was not an option.

To be honest, a lot of tribal Pashtuns from the northwest don't give much importance to good education. It's a belief that has held many of us back. But my father was different. He had an immigrant's mind. He aspired for a better life – for himself and his family. After he moved to Karachi, he realized the importance of education from what he saw in the city.

Karachi is sort of the labouring backbone of Pakistan. No other city can match its incredible work ethic. Nobody works harder than

Karachiites. Nobody pays more taxes than Karachiites. Nobody has been through more trauma and violence than Karachiites. And yes, nobody hits a better square cut than a Karachiite. More on our special batting ability in a bit.

From U-14, the next stage for me was U-16 cricket and that was a whole different story. I was at Federal Secondary till the fifth grade. By grade six, I couldn't concentrate on studying anymore, even if I wanted to. Frankly, I didn't. Even though it was a pretty good private school, offering O-Levels and a co-education, I still wasn't interested in studies. I was quite sure that school – be it private or public – was never my thing. Learning in a static environment was quite disabling. I felt claustrophobic in a classroom; even today I cramp uncomfortably during sit-down instruction lessons with coaches. I don't like tables and chairs and blackboards. Yuck.

So, one day, I decided I'd go to my father and give him an honest deal: pull me out of Federal Secondary and put me in a cheaper, government-run school, where one didn't have to do much, sometimes not even turn up, but where at least the cricket teams were better. I thought I was being honest with him, being open and austere about the choices I wanted to make. I wanted to work on my cricket and not be held back by the high demands and costs of private school, and I didn't want him to spend more than he could afford on my education. I thought that by reasoning with him I would get some appreciation.

Instead, all I got was another beating – a particularly harsh one. My father was angry that I had had the courage to say what I had said to his face. Confronting your elders isn't the Pashtun way, nor is defying their orders. But I meant it all in good faith, and I know that eventually, years later, he realized it.

Life went on. As the war in Afghanistan and the tribal areas came to Karachi and the city grew more violent, it led to what began to be known as Karachi's 'Kalashnikov Culture', inspired by the heavy influx of weapons and narcotics into mainland Pakistan. I remained focused on my game. I took my father's disapproval and his beatings but managed to get into a government school. I didn't have much except my perseverance. Some call it stubbornness. It's still my greatest weapon, I think.

The government-run school had a fantastic cricket team, physically very demanding, and it didn't take me long to join it. I remember it comprised primarily of boys from the ninth and tenth grades. I was the youngest one – a sixth grader – in the team and played inter-school and district-level cricket with the big boys. It was a great honour, my first formal team experience and, like today, I stood out then as well. I was a young kid with a big body. Things worked out.

On the field, I always had a physical advantage. I think it's because of my genes. Pashtuns are built strong and tough. It's the way we are. It's the way many mountain people are. Though not very well schooled like other cricketing greats of Pakistan, my mental strength came from my love for the game – a blinding, unflinching, mad, absolutely crazy love for the game. Day or night, it didn't matter. In those years, after joining the school team, cricket became everything for me. I prayed that I'd keep playing. And playing for me was like praying.

As I gained more confidence in the inter-school and club circuit, any fear of failure began to disappear. My father had tried to instil fear in me about the uncertainty of the game. But you don't feel fear when you're in love. And I was in love with cricket.

My dream, my yardstick for success, was the one and only Khan: Imran. By the time I was in my teens, as he brought home the World Cup in 1992, I dreamt about being like him, his equal. I would pray to God and wonder: 'If Imran Khan has earned so much respect in the eyes of millions everywhere, why can't I? What is holding me back from becoming like him?'

My cricket fever was intense in those days. About three or four nights every week, before I slept, prior to any game or even at practice sessions, I dreamt with my eyes open. I visualized entire matches, all in my head – I'm walking into a stadium, the crowd is cheering, I'm slamming sixes...

I dreamt that I was the new Imran Khan.

I had no option but to dream. As a family, we weren't doing very well at the time. I financed my own cricket kit, bought my own shoes and did what I had to in order to keep playing cricket. There was little help from other members of the family. Sometimes I'd ask my elder brother for cash. Sometimes I'd steal a hundred or five hundred rupees (worth around one to five US dollars today, around twice as much then) from my father's wallet and use it to assemble my kit. Overall, it was a challenging phase in life. And those beatings ... God, I don't think I'll ever forget them. It was passion alone that helped me survive and pursue cricket. Cricket was my fuel. It kept me going.

In those days, the 1990s, playing cricket at the U-14 level in the tough climate of Karachi was a unique experience. I used to sleep with my kit on so that I wouldn't be late for a match the following morning. My shoes would be just under the bed. I'd sleep with my socks on, even in summers, so that I didn't waste time trying to find them in the dark when I awoke at the crack of dawn.

It was in those days that I developed a habit I still struggle with: getting a good night's sleep before a big match. Even when I was captain, I'd arrive early at the ground, usually an hour before anyone else, and just soak in the atmosphere. Even looking at an empty ground helps you understand and plan what you will do. (This habit helped me throughout my career.)

After the morning games, I'd come home and shower and head out in the afternoon for another game, of tape-ball cricket, in the neighbourhood. In the evening, I'd wrap up play just in time to greet my father who would be back from work. To show him that I wasn't all that bad, I'd flip open my books and read aloud, just so that he didn't give me hell about not studying. This routine stuck for more than half the month during the school's calendar year.

The other half of the month was a bit more intense and I would break a few rules. After dark, when everyone at home was in bed, I'd sneak out and jump over the walls of our house to take part in the best part of Karachi cricket – late-night tape-ball tournaments, the pride of Karachi. This was my life: I'd sneak out, play the night match, come back at around four in the morning, exhausted, then wake up at seven for school, and then play the day matches.

It was madness. And I was mad. Cricket mad.

4
THE KARACHI CRICKET CULT

I'M NO cricket historian or master strategist, but I know that every cricket-playing nation has its own culture and subculture, which eventually percolates into the game. The basics matter and become part of your cricketing DNA. They structure your approach and ethics towards the game. Want to know where we get our famous Pakistani aggression from? Read on.

Almost all Pakistani cricketers, the great ones at least, began by playing on the streets with tape and tennis balls. We stand out in this regard. In stark contrast, there are hordes of foreign cricketers who have never played anywhere except at a cricket ground. Does streetside cricket make a difference in how Pakistanis play? Yes, it does.

Firstly, it has made our hand-eye coordination sharper. The tape ball is smaller than a cricket ball and it travels faster and swings a lot more. Thus, as a batsman, you have to be more nimble to attack the ball. Secondly, the tape ball is faster through the air and from the ground. It swings a mile if you shave off the tape from one side.

Importantly, you can play more daring strokes, especially the big, lofted hits.

The concept is pretty simple. A tennis ball, a good one like a Dunlop, is taped up with a single layer of electric tape. Nitto, a Japanese electric tape widely available in Karachi in a variety of colours, was the preferred choice in my days. If the money was too tight for a Dunlop, we would go for a Winn, maybe a Leopard, but you couldn't dip too low; the ball wouldn't have much bounce otherwise. To make things complicated, we sometimes taped them up in multiple colours, but the preferred shades simulated real cricket: red for day matches, white for night.

The taping is done in different ways to stimulate swing and spin, and one can even put in a hard seam in the middle by applying extra tape. The result is a ball that is faster, lighter, moves more in the air and on the ground, and lasts five or six overs on the burning asphalt of a paved Karachi road. Playing with just a tennis ball wouldn't give the extra pace required to simulate a proper cricket ball. Younger kids, however, start with a tennis ball, because it doesn't hurt as much and is slower.

As a tape ball is not as hard as a regular cricket ball, you don't have to pad up, and most windows, street lamps and cars that the ball makes contact with – and it always does – *usually* remain intact. In many ways, tape-ball cricket is the urban cricket fanatic's natural counter-strategy to the lack of proper playing facilities in all major cities of Pakistan. However, every once in a while, you end up with a very angry neighbour with a broken window or a dented bonnet. That's when you have to execute a very good exit plan.

And what if the batsman gets hit on the face or the chest? Well, it doesn't hurt much. A Pathan can certainly take it. Tape chisels your teeth. When you combine the wildly swinging tape ball with the mean streets of central Karachi, where buildings and apartment blocks surround players – creating handicap spots, so you can only score a six over long-on, not long-off, or can only pull over mid-on, not square-leg – your mind develops the ability to work through the gaps like a sniper, not a batsman. It's thrilling to bat on tape. (Till his retirement, Younis Khan practised with a tape ball, shaving it off from half of the ball to play against its consistently crazy swing.)

But this sort of cricket hurts our bowlers. The correct line and length for bowling tape balls is different from the cricket ball. Since it is lighter in weight, one needs to exert more elbow grease while bowling. If you try too hard, you may end up injuring yourself – a common phenomenon. This is possibly why the better bowlers emerge from the Punjab and the northwest. The sprawling landscape, open spaces and parks there allow more room for conventional cricket, unlike the tape-ball cricket in the congested streets of Karachi.

As for the cricket formats we played, there were not a lot to choose from at the time. Even U-14 kids had to play 50-over games. Twenty20 cricket didn't officially exist under the International Cricket Council (ICC) during my growing-up years, but it was fairly common in Karachi's 'Ramadan cricket' circuit. The format is much older and, yes, I can claim that T20 was first invented and played in Karachi during those famous night tournaments held in the city during Ramadan, a time of the year when you can't really play during the day because of the scorching heat and the sixteen hours of fasting.

In fact, in the '90s, T20 cricket was a special 'only-during-Ramadan' feature of the Karachi cricket scene, an annual festival of sorts in the 'City of Lights', as we call it. With a political shake-up happening in the city, gang violence on the rise and stadiums being shutdown or usurped by encroachers, street cricket was the healthiest form of recreation a young man could indulge in. Night cricket and its informal T20 tournaments are a part of the Karachi cricket cult that only a hardcore Karachiite can claim to know of.

They say that necessity is the mother of invention. Indeed, tape-ball cricket is one such invention from Karachi. The urban jungle we grew up in didn't – and still doesn't – have many cricket grounds;

streets, even alleys, therefore serve as proxy playing areas. At any given time of the day, there are all sorts of tape-ball tournaments going on: Apartment Building A versus Apartment Building B, Street 1 versus Street 2, Block X versus Block Y and, of course, at the club versus club level. Although born in Karachi, tape-ball cricket is now quite common in other parts of the country, even the world. In Pakistan, however, it has significantly changed the way cricket is played.

For those of my generation who have grown up on it, tape-ball cricket has created a new breed of cricketers who can do wonders with the ball and bat because of the extra responsiveness the ball demands as well as offers. Puritans say that tape-ball cricket messes up your cricketing skills – especially when it's time for you to play a real game of cricket. I don't agree. Cricket has evolved in the alleys of Karachi just as well as it has in the clubs of Surrey. Its evolution should be welcomed and acknowledged, not shunned.

Any type of cricket, anywhere, is fun. I'm reiterating it: Karachi invented T20 cricket – fuelled by the climate, the number of participating teams, the limited time on our hands and our love for the game.

5

DREAMS, STREET CRED AND A BRUTAL WAKE-UP CALL

PEOPLE DAYDREAM about money and cars. I daydreamed about my shot selection.

My visualization – my habit of staying up at night and thinking about my shots and playing them out in my head, one after the other – has decreased over the years, but it's still there. At one point, I used to play out the whole match in my head, but I don't get anywhere close to that these days.

Back in the day, I would visualize my warm-up, how my body felt, how I felt, how powerful my arm felt, how I released the ball, how it drifted, landed, skidded and spun. For the batting, I would go through my shots and imagine where I would play them, how my legs would feel when I'd shuffle, how my hands would ring after a big shot. I would go through the whole day, motion by motion, one ball after another, in my head.

In the middle of all this, friends came and went. In 1992, when we shifted to Gulshan-e-Iqbal – Block 13, a more upscale neighbourhood than our previous address – it was a different world. The roads were wider, the cricketers I played with were older and more experienced and the tape-ball game was better; tougher actually. Even though it was a bit of a change – there were no Pashtuns or relatives in the area – it didn't matter. There were no politics when it came to cricket, certainly not in my neighbourhood.

That's where I started finding my confidence too, by playing with the older guys and improving my street game while staying a regular in the U-16 circuit. When I entered my teens, I started hanging out late at night with the local hotshots, some gang of friends or the other, some with political connections, doing the things those with 'connections' do. Hanging out after hours on the streets with the guys soon became part of my routine. Then, one day, my elder brother, Tariq, changed it all for me. With a slap.

It was a late night out, when I was chilling with some of the guys, just messing about, when Tariq bhai came and confronted me about how I should be home once the match was over. When I protested, he slapped me – in front of everyone.

I felt so small, embarrassed and angry. Tariq bhai had insulted me by hitting me in public. He also warned me that while he encouraged my playing cricket – he too had played cricket at the first-class level and was, in fact, a very good fast bowler – he didn't approve of the social habits I'd embraced on the side.

I was incensed that he had insulted me in front of everyone. But it was only years later that I realized the importance of what he had done. Not only did I deserve that slap, I was also glad that he gave it to me in public. Had I continued associating with those people, in those heady years of being a teen in central Karachi, I'm sure I would have lost my focus on cricket. Many of the guys I hung out with didn't end up doing too well.

Here's the thing about being young. At that age, you always think you're right and nobody else 'gets it' but you. It's you versus the world. But I've learnt the hard way that our elders are always thinking about the big picture, about the larger issues in life, which you can't see as a youngster who is well-intentioned but too self-involved.

That's what that slap was. As a cricketer, Tariq bhai could have been as legendary as Imran Khan for me. I believed he was *that* good. More importantly, he was also the wall between my father and me, and encouraged and protected my cricketing pursuits from my disapproving father. If he had hurt me, he had done so for a reason.

6
ALL THE WORLD IS A STOCK MARKET

THE MOVE to a new neighbourhood also meant a change of club. From Shadab Sports, I now joined Total Energy. Here the well-known former cricketer Aftab Ahmad was very supportive, as were the others, like Achay bhai, Bokhari sahib and Salahuddin Sallu – all local legends. By that time, I was playing regularly in the U-16 and U-19 tournaments, and was doing pretty well on the Karachi cricket circuit.

I was still coming in to bat at number seven or eight and getting 50s and 60s here and there, but it was my bowling that was really beginning to take off. I was scooping five- and six-wicket hauls in almost every game. An outcome of this was that observers, coaches and the local scouts didn't think much of my batting. They always thought I was a bowler and so did I. This would become a recurring reason for both belief and doubt in equal measure about my cricketing speciality, in the years that followed. I had no idea what lay ahead for me.

Eventually, the consistency with the ball paid off. I took my first step towards the big leagues when my name came up in the list of U-19 probables for an international tour to the West Indies. Haroon Rasheed was a selector at the time and the dynamic Mohammad Wasim was the captain. On a blazing hot afternoon in Karachi, I was called for a trial. I passed. I wasn't nervous or edgy. In fact, I was raring to go, ready and eager to be on my first foreign cricket tour. Moreover, this would be the first time I'd leave Pakistani soil and set foot in another country.

I want to share something here that I have never disclosed before. It's something that's very personal and will help you understand my thought process and approach towards cricket a lot better. It's a story about my roots, my fears and my focus.

My father, a reasonably successful entrepreneur by then had, thanks to someone's advice, invested a lot of money in the stock market. However, one day, when the markets crashed, as they always do, he lost a huge amount – around 10 million rupees (equivalent to around a hundred thousand dollars today, and around a quarter of a million dollars then) in a single day.

I still remember the day it happened. At the time we had a new house in Gulshan. We had a car too, along with all the modest luxuries a family needed. Things were going well and I was doing better and better at cricket. And then, suddenly, the markets tanked. Tragedy struck and everything changed overnight.

What hurt me more – more than the beatings I received at the hands of my father – was to see him and my mother sit on the prayer rug and weep at night. Tariq bhai, who was my rock, also broke down often and wondered how we would ever make up for the loss. That was possibly the worst phase we endured as a family. Remember: there were eleven of us. How would my sisters get married? How would we finish our education? Those were some questions to which there weren't any easy answers anymore. As a family, we would never talk about money. But now that the situation was grim, my parents even considered selling our house – and it still wouldn't have been enough. Frankly, we were out of options. I felt the dull stab of uncertainty and poverty as we started rationing our food and cut down our expenses significantly.

Emotionally, our spirits had hit rock bottom, especially when I'd sneak up on my parents and see them weeping, looking heavenwards, asking the Almighty for help. I'd see them do this every night. It broke my heart to hear their sobs. Later, when I'd go and touch the prayer rugs after they were in bed, I'd find them soaked with their tears.

That's when I prayed for just one thing. I prayed to God – all I wanted was to play for Pakistan, if only to help my parents get out of the hell they were in. I was not well schooled and too young to work in an office or anywhere where they would pay me a decent sum. My only hope, for my family and its problems, was to excel at cricket.

Our family's struggle and the phase of uncertainty continued for a few months, and then, just like that, I received a call-up for Pakistan 'A'. And then, soon after, for the Pakistan national team. Life changed overnight. I started believing in the power of prayer and have never stopped since.

I will never forget those days. Never. After all, those were some of the darkest days my family ever saw. We belonged to a humble background and had built a modest existence for ourselves through some years of struggle in Karachi. Losing it all suddenly had really shocked and affected us all. It broke down everything around us – everything except my game.

I didn't let my game be affected. I didn't have the option of failing. When I decided that I would help my family overcome its trauma through cricket, making it to the top of the game became the only option. There was no other choice.

Honestly, my plan was naïve. Those days, there wasn't much money in cricket, even at the highest level. When I eventually made it to the national side in 1996, we were paid around 9,000–10,000 rupees (two hundred US dollars then, around a hundred US dollars now) per game. It wasn't a large sum at the time and I couldn't seriously think that I would dramatically turn around my family's fortunes with my match fees. So it wasn't the cash I was headed for. (That came much later, when the game changed in the new millennium and became more popular and commercialized.)

I was headed for stability. I needed it, my family needed it. I needed to do well for them, especially my father, and not be a burden to him. So I kept on playing – I had no other area of focus, nor did I have any other hopes or aspirations. The only skills I had lay in cricket.

Maybe it was the blind hopefulness and naiveté of being a kid. Maybe it was sheer willpower. But I believed that if God had put me in a crisis, then He would bail me out of it as well. All I wanted was to play for Pakistan. Nothing else.

And when God decided to bail me out, His help came at full speed – like a fast, bouncy delivery, ready to smash your face if you don't dispatch it for a six. I received God's help, graciously, head-on.

7

A FIRST, A TRIAL, THEN
ANOTHER FIRST

I CAN'T forget the day it happened. Receiving a call-up to play for one's country is a feeling and memory that's right up there with the emotions one feels on the day one's child is born.

I was in the West Indies on tour with the Pakistan 'A' U-19. The tour began well – for starters, it was my first trip out of Pakistan and that was the case for most of my fellow teammates as well. Many of us had stepped into an aircraft for the first time. There was more excitement than fear. We were really pumped and wanted to do well. On that tour, we would bump into many Windies U-19 players who would become stars for their national side in the coming years: Wavell Hinds, Ramnaresh Sarwan, Reon King, to name a few. The exposure was great. But, as expected on a first tour, there were some challenges.

Firstly, we couldn't find *halal* or kosher food anywhere. Secondly, the chicken – and boy, the Windies love their chicken – we got served had pieces as large as footballs. I remember I ended up overeating and vomited the first day. So, getting the right kind of food was a major struggle. (Our coach, Haroon Rasheed, eventually figured a way out of the *halal* food crisis.) Still, everything was big in the West Indies – big men, big women, big chicken pieces...

We were still coming to terms with the country, its food and its people when there was a scandal – an allegation of rape against Zeeshan Pervaiz, one of the batsmen in our team. The police had got involved too and things got quite ugly. According to Zeeshan, a woman, much older than him, had tried to entrap him. Though frankly, I felt both were at fault. There's no real way of explaining this and defending him, except by saying that he was young, inexperienced – both in terms of travelling and women – and it was his first international tour.

Zeeshan and I had a bit of a history. A couple of days before his scandal became known, the two of us had had an argument and a subsequent falling-out. We were not on talking terms and everyone in the team knew about this. After the scandal, however, when the police got involved and things became quite serious, I got really disturbed by it all. I couldn't sleep much. I went to Haroon Rasheed in the middle of the night, broke down in front of him and begged him to save Zeeshan. I felt terrible that a fellow teammate I had had a war of words with over some stupid locker-room row was now in deep trouble.

Zeeshan and I were quite opposites when it came to our cricket, particularly our batting. He was a classic, orthodox batsman. I was certain that he had a bright future ahead of him. Maybe it was our altercation that made me step up and try to be a hero or something. I volunteered and became a witness on his behalf, ready to say that it was the woman's fault entirely, even though I didn't know much about what had happened between them and I doubted him too.

So, there I was, ready to falsely testify to save a teammate. I know it may sound terrible and immature, even dishonest, to admit to it today, but I was just a kid who wanted to stand up for a mate who had obviously screwed up and had a lot to lose in terms of future prospects. It's what young men have always done for other young men in battle and in trouble, even if it doesn't sound right or make any sense. It's just the way some of us are. It's ridiculously childish behaviour but that's the thing: we were children and we thought we were right.

Eventually, thank God, there was no need for my testimony. It all worked out for Zeeshan – the court in Kingston acquitted him for lack of evidence. Though I'm not morally comfortable about it today, I was very proud then to have offered to help out a teammate in trouble. My motives were, without a doubt, well intentioned, even though the act – never committed by me – was, allegedly, a dishonourable one. Thank God for the West Indies judiciary.

As for the series, it went on as per schedule. I remember, in Barbados I picked up 22 wickets in three matches and put some solid runs on the board too. Things were going well for me on the field. Eventually, from the mix of one-day and three-day matches, we would win two, lose two and draw five.

Then, one morning, I was brushing my teeth and getting ready for the day's game when Haroon Rasheed called me and said, 'Congratulations, Shahid. Your name has come up for consideration for the Pakistan team.'

I don't know if it was the earth that moved beneath my feet or if I was shaken to the core. But on hearing him say those words, I was stunned. My toothbrush, still in my mouth, remained there, frozen. All I could reply, in sheer disbelief, was a muffled, 'What?!'

It was a genuine question. Amidst the scandal and the excitement of our own series, I hadn't kept track of happenings in the national team. On tour in Africa, the Pakistani team was hurting in Kenya. Mushtaq Ahmed, the best spinner in the side – maybe in the world at the time – was injured. Considering my recent performance in the series in West Indies, I had been selected to replace him.

When Haroon Rasheed called to tell me about it, I initially thought he was joking, although I was too scared to ask if he was. But once he told me the boring details – travel, paperwork – I realized he was serious. When he began telling me about my next steps – catching the right flights, picking up some gear from Karachi and joining the national team in Kenya – my immediate reaction was fear. I was terrified. How would I deal with the pressure? Would I play with the likes of Wasim Akram, Waqar Younis and Inzamam-ul-Haq? Weren't they supposed to give you prior notice and prepare you before calling you to join the national team? Didn't you have to attend a class or two? Weren't they supposed to give you more time? But wait: this was my dream since I was a kid. So why was I scared? Wasn't this the realization of my dream, to hang out with these legends in the dressing room, play alongside them, be one of them, be like them? Then why was I terrified?

My next move, making a phone call home, only added to my apprehensions. My family couldn't believe the news either. When I told them that I was cutting the Windies tour short and coming back to Pakistan and then heading to Kenya to join the national side, they didn't take my word for it. They suspected that I had got myself into some legal trouble due to the Zeeshan Pervaiz controversy. Tariq bhai actually called the coach to confirm if I was telling the truth. So much for my credibility with my family!

8

THE INSOMNIAC'S DREAM
DEBUT

AFTER THE initial excitement wore off, my maiden tour to the West Indies was all about fear and introspection. Of course, I was just a young boy and excited to be in the position I was in. But I was quite apprehensive about my father's financial situation. I was scared about what would happen to my family if I didn't succeed. Every time I walked out of the dressing room to the field, my family's near-bankruptcy played on my mind.

When we U-19 players boarded that flight from Karachi, we were just *londas* and *laparas* – boys and sloggers. Many of us hadn't even seen the inside of an aircraft till then. After flying for hours, when we landed in the Caribbean and faced obstacles and scandals and endured them together, those interactions and experiences turned into lifelong friendships, not just amongst the Pakistani bunch, but also our opponents on the tour – Sarwan, Hinds, Gayle, King. What a great first tour for a bunch of young boys!

However, after that 'toothbrush call' by Haroon Rasheed, nothing was the same anymore. Too bad my folks suspected my involvement in the Zeeshan Pervaiz controversy – they thought I was being grounded and sacked. Yet, everything after that call is today a blur, and for good reason.

I remember the difficult itinerary: Barabados to Guyana, Guyana to London, London to Dubai, Dubai to Karachi, one hour in Karachi – with just a few minutes with my family, who got me my gear – and then from Karachi back to Dubai, and then off to Nairobi. By the time I boarded the flight for Nairobi, I was too tired to sleep. I did not sleep for a minute. How could I? All I was thinking of – the only thing I could – was how, in a few hours, I was going to be with the very guys every Pakistani kid knew about and wanted to emulate. What would meeting them be like? How would the dressing room be? Would Wasim Akram indeed be as tall as I'd heard he was? How strong would Waqar Younis's handshake be? How big was Inzi? Would these names I'd grown up dreaming about be nice to me? Or would they be mean and curt? Would they even acknowledge me, a teenager? Would I be picked on? Would there be an initiation into the team? Honestly, I couldn't deal with it. By the time I landed in Nairobi, I was tired, but full of excitement and anticipation.

The first Pakistani player I met was Aamer Sohail, the aggressive left-hander, in the lobby of the hotel we were put up in. Sohail would become the first teammate to bond and connect with me. (It's a pity that in the years that followed, he'd become the first Pakistan player I'd have a falling-out with.)

Next, near the elevators, I bumped into Saqlain Mushtaq, one of the younger guys in the squad. I had no idea that day that over the years, we would become great friends, even competitors. Soon after, I met Wasim (Akram) bhai. Even today, my first impression of him is extremely positive: What a guy! What a great leader! What a towering and benevolent man! On that first day with the team, I had no inkling of how important a role he would play in my career, how he would become my biggest mentor, both on and off the field.

Everybody I met was very welcoming, especially Moin (Khan) bhai, who would eventually become my yardstick of morale and teambuilding. He has a lot of *rakh rakhao*, as we call it: the desi ability to be a proper gentleman. He became my first true friend in the team. Of course, the friendly, buddy vibe developed over time. But on that first day, I was star-struck. Everybody around me was a star. In fact, all members of that team – Saeed Anwar (captain), Saleem Elahi, Ijaz Ahmed, Ramiz Raja, Saleem Malik, Moin Khan, Saqlain Mushtaq, Waqar Younis, Shahid Nazir and others – were superstars. The current Pakistan team, in 2019, has just one or two. That Pakistan team, in 1996, was full of them.

The best part, however, was that I wasn't scared or nervous about being on the big stage anymore. Nor was I underconfident. I stopped being a bundle of nerves, even though I thought I'd be one when I'd meet my teammates. Moreover, everything happened so quickly that I forgot to wear the Pakistan blazer – in fact, there had been no time to get one stitched. I was still wearing my U-19 jacket. And yet, there I was, part of one of the greatest teams ever to play the great game.

Also, for the record, I was just nineteen, and not sixteen like they claim. I was born in 1977. So, yes, the authorities stated my age incorrectly, and there's a reason for it.

I was born in a village, that too in a house, not a hospital. There was no birth certificate. There were no doctors. Record keeping wasn't a thing in the rural northwest in the Pakistan of the 1970s. I'm from a culture where our elders told us if we were born in the summer, the rainy season, or in winter. That's how things remained, informal and anecdotal, till years later, standing in line to register for an U-14 cricket camp in Karachi, I was asked about my age by a selector. Embarrassingly, at that precise moment, I remembered only the day and month – 1 March – but not the year of my birth. Seeing my confusion, a fellow mate standing in the same line with me, advised me to state a year. Without thinking, I blurted it out to the selector. He believed me. From there on, I was in the cricketing ecosystem, but with the incorrect age against my name.

To be sure, in 1996, after my formal induction into the Pakistan team, the discrepancy about my age began to bother me, especially considering the hype around my century in Nairobi. Initially, I'd even shared my concern with my Pakistan teammates but such conversations didn't go beyond the dressing room.

It was only years later, when I returned to Khyber Pakhtunkhwa that I could establish my correct year of birth. Once I had confirmation, I knew that I must, for the record, state my correct age – for my fans and for the game. This here, 1 March 1977, is my correct date of birth.

Back to Nairobi: when I got to meet the rest of the squad, surprisingly, everybody was warm. The seniors – Moin Khan, Wasim Akram, Ramiz Raja – were very caring in a do-you-need-anything kind of way. They saw me during practice; it was the first time they all saw me bat. They backed me up, cheered me on and gave me great tactical advice. At the time, Saqlain Mushtaq was also a newcomer in the team. So was Azhar Mahmood. I adjusted quickly with the younger guys. The fear factor quickly vanished into a manageable comfort zone. Being the youngest was actually an advantage. My roommate on that tour of Kenya was the classy leftie, Shadab Kabir. We had some good times together.

Closer to match day for my debut, the nets started. I remember when they told me to pad up. I couldn't believe what started happening. I faced Wiqi bhai (Waqar Younis), Wasim bhai, even the first-class legend, Saqlain Mushtaq, and pounded them away on all sides of the nets. My shots were big and natural, and came hard and quick. I had switched on my batting and had switched off any edgy nerves.

My famous century's roots lie in those nets sessions. Here's a confession: all bowlers really like to bat. I was inducted into the national side as a bowler and was really looking forward to batting in the nets. In fact, I thought it was the only batting I'd get on the tour. So when the nets started, I did my thing. I slammed everything. I was free, not nervous, and started going after every ball – even those from Wasim Akram and Waqar Younis.

Naturally, my slam-bam hitting at the nets didn't go unnoticed. The next day, the two Ws made some sort of pact, which was based around skinning me. Both of them upped their pace by a few notches. But I didn't feel it and I didn't care – I hit them all around anyway. The faster they came at me, the harder I hit back. I wasn't trying to prove anything. I was just trying to play my natural game. I had no apprehensions or any pressure.

Then, after the nets came the rumour every batsman waits for the locker-room mill to churn out – that he might open the innings. Soon, the confirmation came in. Wasim bhai, before he headed back to Pakistan to deal with a family emergency, had told Saeed Anwar – he was to lead the team in his absence – to make sure I batted. I will always be thankful to him for believing in me.

But opening the innings for Pakistan? It was as unbelievable as it was unlikely. Outwardly, I was a bit hesitant ('Listen, I've come as a bowler, I don't think I can do this'). Of course, secretly, I welcomed it. Cricket is about adventure and risks. And international cricket is the greatest adventure of all.

The scenario built up somewhat like this. I never batted in the first match, my ODI debut, against Kenya. It wasn't a bad game and I had a decent spell, starting proceedings in the 17th or 18th over, and even grabbed a catch off Saqlain's bowling. I didn't get to bat during our innings. However, I didn't have much to worry about in that match. My teammates backed me and I'd done well in the West Indies. Kenya, with all due respect, was not the strongest opposition in the world at the time.

Before the second match, all I'd been told was, 'Listen, you may be opening tomorrow, or going in one down.'

When we all turned in for the night, I couldn't get my wits together. But anyway, I slept, or tried to sleep. I was thoroughly fidgety and very anxious. I remember when I thought it was time to wake up, I went to the washroom, showered and shaved and woke up my roommate, Shadab Kabir.

He said, 'What's wrong, Lala?'

I said, 'Time for the game, man. Let's go!'

Shadab responded, 'Lala, have you gone mad? It's two-thirty in the morning! Get some sleep!'

I was embarrassed. Tired of waiting, I tried to sleep again. When I woke up, I apologized to Shadab for having woken him up earlier. Then we started talking.

'I had a dream last night,' I told him.

'How could you? You didn't sleep!' he said, jokingly.

'I'm serious. I had a dream that I was slamming Jayasuriya and Muralitharan and Dharmasena for sixes,' I said. 'Big, huge sixes.'

'Let's pray it happens, brother,' said Shadab. 'Now, let's get some breakfast.'

The dream and how it came true – Jayasuriya went for 94 off his 10 overs, and Muralitharan went for 73 – is something Shadab talks to me about even today. He remembers it because he was the only one I'd shared that moment with. In cricket, roommates end up sharing memories together. That was our moment. It was a dream that God willed. Its coming true was also something He willed, and it has remained with me as a precious memory since then.

In that match, Saeed Anwar and Saleem Elahi opened with the bat. They had a good start. Elahi got out when the scorecard read 60. I went in at number three.

There is an interesting Indian connection to my innings in that match. Sachin Tendulkar had given his favourite bat to Waqar Younis and asked for a favour. Sachin wanted Waqar to take the bat to Sialkot, Pakistan's world-famous sports-good manufacturing capital, and get a custom-made one replicated there. Wiqi bhai was thus the custodian of Sachin's great, favourite blade. But guess what Waqar did before he took it to Sialkot? He gave it to me, before I went in to bat. So effectively, I scored that first century in Nairobi with Sachin Tendulkar's best bat. Go figure.

People say that what happened in the match itself was remarkable and historic, but for me, it really wasn't. I remember the sequence but only mechanically. I padded up. I went in. I stopped the first ball. Then I hit the second ball for a six. After that, I don't remember much about what unfolded. Whatever came my way, I played it on its merit. If a ball was worth hitting, it got the required treatment.

It didn't bother me that Saeed Anwar was at the other end. Saeed is a legend and my favourite fellow batsman from that time, a stylish leftie whose strokeplay I keenly watched when the matches aired on TV. But his presence at the non-striker's end didn't unsettle me. Nor do I have anything significant to say about the fact that my innings was a landmark moment in cricket history. I didn't feel the gravity of the moment while batting. Facing the great Muttiah Muralitharan, Sanath Jayasuriya and Chaminda Vaas – all champions from Sri Lanka's 1996 World Cup-winning team – felt normal, too. It felt like a first-class or a club-cricket regulation game for me. Maybe I wasn't mature enough to understand what was going on. In that ground, at that moment, I felt like this was what I had always done and this was what I would always do.

Some say that my century in Nairobi that day, 4 October 1996, changed the way the modern game would be played. I won't pretend I did something remarkable – it didn't seem that way to me. I don't think I changed anything, nor did I perform in any special way or with any strategic plan in that innings. For me, my rhythm, my style – it was all my normal, regular approach towards batting. Maybe that's why I don't remember much of that innings. It was all standard hitting. Karachi had just met Nairobi, and while the latter was shocked, the former was just fine. Of course, Karachi wanted to prove a point.

But a couple of moments in that innings do stick out. Murali was in his prime at the time and known for being a crafty, sudden turner of the ball. So hitting him for a six – and I think I hit him for three or four sixes – was especially satisfying. My timing was better than it had ever been in those shots off Murali. In Pashto, we have a saying about hunting: the bigger the prey, the tastier the meal. I was taking the saying very seriously.

While at the crease, I didn't know I was setting a record. I only found out when I got back to the dressing room and Ramiz Raja told me, 'You've just set up a world record, partner.' I didn't take it that seriously. Numbers don't make sense to me – they never did and never will. Unlike a lot of cricketers, keeping up with statistics and records, generally or even my own, has never been my thing. I did ask, though, what the record was, just to be sure, and Ramiz said that it was for the fastest century ever, and I was also the youngest player to do so.

I still don't make much of it. In Nairobi, at the time, there was not a lot of local news coverage to read or watch. That probably helped me stay in my bubble. Later, after the match, I hung out with Moin Khan in his room. A fellow Karachiite, he was really happy for me and told me what a big deal it was that I had managed to pull off a century in 37 balls. He broke down my performance as a teammate, a spectator, even a coach. But I still didn't realize the gravity of what I had just done. It was all happening too fast. I was just happy to have the opportunity of playing with my favourite cricketers – and Pakistan's finest – against the world champions that year.

It was only after the tour, when we returned to Pakistan, that I was forced to change my mind. There were thousands of supporters at Karachi's Jinnah International Airport who came to see me, probably to catch a glimpse of a random Pathan kid from Gulshan who had created a world record out of nowhere. The song and dance at the airport, the flowers they threw at me, the way they carried me on their shoulders and hugged and kissed me – it was their warmth, pride and love that made me realize what I had done.

That's when it hit me. That's when it all started to make sense. I had indeed done something serious, something big, even historic. Not the century itself. Not the praise in the dressing room. Not the late-night chat with Moin.

It was getting off that flight that changed everything – my game, my life, my family's future. More than anything, it changed my own perception of myself.

But the future wasn't as rosy as that welcome at Karachi Airport made me think it would be.

9
THE QUEST BEGINS

IN RETROSPECT, I'm one of the few who played the game and just kept going. Most cricketers quit after a decade. I got two solid ones in.

It's been over twenty years at the international level and I'm still playing – now in other limited-overs formats. I praise God for giving me the strength and good health to continue. There were several occasions when I wanted to stop. There were times when my body wanted me to stop. There were moments when my hand–eye coordination was all out of place. There were days when I looked at my daughters – Aqsa, Ansha, Ajwa and Asmara – and only wanted to spend more time with them. There was also that terrible phase after my father passed away.

Thankfully, these were all moments that came and went. (By the way, I still try to spend all the time I can with my children.)

After my debut series in Kenya, everything – the attention, the cricket, the energy and the zing – went into overdrive. Next up that winter was a triangular series Down Under featuring Australia, West

Indies and Pakistan – the Carlton and United Series. It would be my first tour of Australia.

The Mark Taylor–led Australia side that year had made it to the finals of the World Cup but were in trouble in that series. They won their first couple of games and then things went south. So, it was the West Indies we met in the double-final. Their performance had been the exact opposite of the Aussies: they lost their first couple of games, and then pulled up their socks and surged ahead to take us and the Aussies head-on.

As for Pakistan, we were either terrible or brilliant – the usual traits in our cricket. That series was the first time I bowled my faster one – I think Greg Blewett was the first victim – and the Aussie commentators were all over me. My batting in the series – I was 'Man of the Finals' – earned me the name 'Kid Dynamite' in the Australian press, way before India's Ravi Shastri coined the more permanent 'Boom Boom'. But clearly, it was Saqlain Mushtaq who dominated the series and introduced his own version of the *doosra*, the one that spun the other way, years before Muralitharan would. On that tour, both Saqlain and I, young, unbridled, creative, had our original tricks and techniques to counter the opposition: Down Under, Saqi and I were a proper duo.

I remember the first final, a low-scoring game, where we were chasing 180. I opened the innings with Inzamam and hit 53 off 54. Ian Bishop, Curtly Ambrose and Courtney Walsh were part of the Windies pace battery. It was the first time I was playing such an all-star bowling attack, that too on Australia's seamer-friendly pitches. Moreover, there was a lot of pressure on us in that game, and it had nothing to do with the Windies' ferocious bowling attack.

This new stage fright was self-inflicted. A day prior to that game, Saqlain and I had had a 'night out' (read party) with a senior player whom I won't name. But much to our surprise, this unnamed player spilled the beans about our evening to the skipper, Wasim Akram, who became livid on learning that we had 'broken curfew and stepped out'.

Here's the thing about Wasim Akram: he is a thorough gentleman. Every time he meets you, the first 90 seconds are nothing but an exchange of pleasantries. He will inquire about you, your family and your health. He is not someone who raises his voice, nor does he ever get straight to business.

But that day, on the morning of the first final, he really gave us an earful. Our only excuse was the late start to the game – it was a day-night match – and that the senior player had said it was okay to step out. But Wasim bhai didn't want to hear any of our excuses. He was firm and laid down the law: if we didn't perform that day, there would be no place for us in the team in the future. So, clearly, with the most well-known Windies attack in history glaring at me from down the pitch and Wasim's ultimatum at the back of my mind, it was crucial that I score well in that game. In some ways, it was a do-or-die situation for me.

After Wasim bhai's reprimand, Saqlain and I chatted and decided that we had to give our best. There was no way out. Saqlain did all right with his bowling. I did well with both the ball (3 for 33 in 10 overs) and the bat (53 off 54 balls, 8x4). That was also the day I fought off the myth around the West Indies pace attack – in Pakistan we call it the *kaali aandhi*, the black storm. Although a racial description, it's not meant as a racist comment and is fondly used in the Pakistan press.

Anyway, moral of the story: do not party with your teammates the night before a big match. If you do, make sure you kick some ass the next day and win. Wasim bhai's ultimatum stuck: from that day, both Saqlain and I stopped partying the night before a match. That didn't mean we stopped partying altogether. More on that in just a bit.

Since I mentioned that it's important to kick ass, I must share a related story. In that first final, I also caught and bowled Brian Lara.

Yup. Brian Charles Lara TC, OCC, AM from Santa Cruz, Trinidad, caught and bowled by the nineteen-year-old Shahid Afridi from the streets of Gulshan-e-Iqbal, Karachi.

Lara was a bit of a myth and nightmare (particularly for bowlers) at the time. But we dealt with him in our own way. There was a hit Indian film song in those days, '*Koi jae to le aye*', that was quite popular in Pakistan too. We Pakistani players had made our own rendition of the item number which featured one of the hot favourite actors at the time, Mamta Kulkarni. At the chorus she would move to the words '*Maara re*', and we would sing something on the lines of '*Maara re, Lara ne mujh ko maara re* (I've been hit, oh I've been hit by Lara)', in the dressing room whenever we were playing the Windies. That's how awesome Lara was: he had inspired the entire Pakistan team to dedicate a not-so-original Bollywood soundtrack to him!

But to me, Lara's wicket was a big deal because I was still in my teens, he was twenty-seven, averaging over 47 in ODIs, and had played more than a hundred matches. Basically, he was at his peak and I was a rookie, only on my second international tour. And we were playing against each other at the prestigious Sydney Cricket Ground.

I remember charging in. I remember him volleying it back to me, low. I remember going for it. The rest was just instinct and automated hand–eye coordination. But I think I figured out there, mid-dive, before I hit the turf, that we now had the match in our grasp. I was right. What a rush it was! What a way to get the greatest batsman of the era!

So there I was, in Australia and on a roll. That crazy 102 in Kenya. A killer series Down Under. In a few months, I'd graduated from skirmishing in the locker room with Zeeshan Pervaiz to claiming Brian Lara's scalp. Life had changed. Forever.

The best bit about my life in those early days wasn't the cricket, though. It was returning home. The crowds at the airport, the love and affection I'd get the minute I landed till the time I reached home, made me realize whom I was playing for: my people, my family. Their happiness was all that mattered.

At the time, I hadn't begun looking at things from a commercial perspective. But all of a sudden, there were a lot of sponsors interested in me. Of course, there was plenty of attention from all quarters – especially women – but all I was really interested in was helping my family, especially my father, recover from the terrible loss he had suffered. Financially and emotionally, I wanted to be there for him. He'd been a successful man all his life and a financial loss of that stature had dealt a big blow to his self-confidence. So I wanted to make sure my parents and siblings had two square meals a day, and that my father recovered his sense of self-belief and independence. That's all.

That's why I was playing cricket – two square meals a day and some self-respect.

That's all one needs anyway.

10

PATHAN VS HINDUSTAN

1996, THE year I debuted, was a happening one.

First, Sri Lanka beat Australia comprehensively and won the final of the World Cup at Lahore by seven wickets. Then, Dada and The Wall arrived: Sourav Ganguly and Rahul Dravid both debuted in Test cricket, with scores of 131 and 96, respectively. The legendary Dickie Bird umpired his last Test at Lord's. And Wasim bhai, at his peak, took his 300th Test wicket.

The following year, Pakistan's 50th year of Independence, I visited India for the first time to play the Independence Cup, a quadrangular ODI tournament featuring Sri Lanka, New Zealand, Pakistan and the hosts.

With my smashing debut and the successful Australia tour under my belt at the start of the year, I knew I was in for a thrilling ride. Playing in the hot summer months in India wasn't ideal, but most of the games were day-night matches and we weren't going to let the weather get in the way of our trying to beat India at home.

Too bad India got their car keys handed to them early in that series. They beat the Kiwis in one game and were demolished by both Sri Lanka and Pakistan. Our team didn't feature Wasim bhai, Waqar bhai and the wily Mushtaq Ahmed – all three were busy playing county cricket in England. Without three of the game's greatest bowlers, our bowling looked weak on paper. But we were not weak-willed.

Ramiz bhai was captain of the side. We played in our famous light-green jerseys, my favourite kit over all these years. The hype around the tournament was insane. As for me, I wanted the great Indian experience: movie stars, the Taj Mahal and bhel puri. But more than anything else, I wanted Pakistan to beat India in all our games in that series.

As for the welcome and fanfare, it was unrelenting and unprecedented. I wasn't expecting what I got in India, honestly. The way we were followed around by the press, the way the fans used to wait near hotel elevators for hours to see us … It's true – India really is the modern hub of international cricket. The sport is a religion, a cult, a state within the state and a way of life in that country. I was overwhelmed and simply blown away.

But there were mistakes. In our first match of the tournament in Mohali, we were naïve to put the Kiwis in to bat – we thought they wouldn't be able to beat the heat. Bad move. Nathan Astle, the right-handed opener and medium pacer, cost us 117 runs before he was stumped off my bowling. Chasing 286, we tried hard but eventually lost by 22 runs, failing to build on the momentum I had provided as opener (59 off 46, 4x4, 2x6).

During the next match in Gwalior, a city once ruled by Pathans, Saeed Anwar and I ran a number at the top of the order. We would help put up a solid total and offer a dynamic start – made fashionable in 1996 by the famous Sri Lankan opening duo of Sanath Jayasuriya and Romesh Kaluwitharana – against the world champions themselves. Saeed was the sane mainstay of our opening partnership (32 off 60) and I went a bit off the rails on the other end (52 off 29, 9x4, 2x6). I hadn't done much with the ball in that series till then, but was pleased to see that Saeed and I had developed a good chemistry as Pakistan's opening combination. We put up 289 on board – a massive total in those times, unlike today, when even 300-plus cannot guarantee a win. The Lankans, who had gained a reputation of being smart chasers, fell short by 30 runs.

Finally, in the heat wave of north India, Pakistan had marked their arrival in the series.

Soon it was time for our third match, against India. I'd waited for that moment for a long time.

For me, the India story begins with the six that Javed Miandad had hit off Chetan Sharma in Sharjah in 1986. That stroke not only cleared the fence and won Pakistan the match in incredible style, but also captured the imagination of millions of Pakistanis and Indians for years. It became a psychological benchmark for Pakistan. It wasn't any ordinary shot, because it made clear whenever comparisons were drawn between India and Pakistan that Pakistan was the better team. Period. Eventually, over the years, the Indians would improve – vastly – but Javed bhai's six is so memorable that even today it continues to give Pakistan some extra momentum whenever the team plays in the UAE (United Arab Emirates). Such was the impact and obsession with that match's outcome that there was even a commemorative rhyme that was taught at school, documenting that last shot.

The desert was burning
Chetan was bowling
Javed was batting
Runs required: four
This had never happened before
Chetan bowled a strange ball
It never touched the ground at all
You know what happened to that ball?
It went straight into the VIP Hall!

After that great six, Pakistan became the *badshah* of every tournament held in Sharjah and our domination against India at the same venue continued for several years. This track record built up my India obsession even more. As a young boy, I didn't have the means to travel to see any of those games. But on television I don't think I missed even a single India–Pakistan match.

But there was baggage, too. There was, of course, our defeat in the 1996 World Cup quarterfinal in Bangalore at the back of my mind. (I hadn't received a call-up for the national side at that stage, but had seen our batting collapse in that match.) After having won the previous edition Down Under in 1992, crashing out in the quarterfinals was a sad moment for Pakistan. Also, it was another bloody World Cup loss to India – a jinx that has now spawned even television commercials whenever the teams face off in ICC tournaments. It's Pakistan's very own Curse of the Bambino, though I'm confident we won't take as long to break it as the Boston Red Sox did.

Thus, as far as India–Pakistan matches were concerned, I was just like any other fan from the two nations – fanatical about the rivalry. But in those days, before the commercialization of cricket really took off, the hype about India–Pak games was real, not superficial or drummed up by social and mainstream media. We felt it on the field as the players faced each other in the middle. The rivalry was raw and genuine, not politicized and commercialized.

In my first match versus India, I disappointed myself more than anyone else. I had a single-digit score next to my name. Nothing much with the ball, either, except catching Rahul Dravid off Aaqib Javed.

But I remember it all clearly. We were in Chennai. I opened with Saeed Anwar. The crowd's roar was the loudest noise I'd ever heard; I felt the earth shaking and I swear I couldn't feel my bat. I'm not sure if I could even see the bowler properly. To be honest, I was scared and hoping that the first ball would come and just pass – off and away. I was at the crease for some nine minutes only, scoring just five off six balls. I wasn't surprised to get out early (caught Sourav Ganguly, bowled Abey Kuruvilla). I remember my head and heart pounding throughout that day. My head, because of the heat, and my heart, because of the noise. Oh, that noise. The sheer noise of the world's greatest rivalry.

But despite getting out early, I would remain in the game. Something unusual happened in that match – an important milestone in Pakistan's and South Asia's cricket history. Something that let the game go on to become one of the greatest matches ever played between India and Pakistan, and I would be in the centre of it.

A few minutes after my dismissal when I was back in the pavilion, I was asked to return to the middle to run for Saeed Anwar, who was injured but still batting well. He was dehydrated thanks to the extreme humidity in Chennai. When he was at 50 or 60, he began to experience severe cramps too.

For Saeed bhai and for Pakistan, I ran a lot that day. It was rough for me – and I ran for almost three hours – and can't imagine how it was for Saeed; he was there for 206 minutes. The heat and humid weather were crazy. But so was the atmosphere, and Saeed bhai was in great touch. He just kept connecting bat to ball, non-stop. By the time he was in the middle of his mammoth 194, setting up what would become a world record for years – beating Viv Richards's thirteen-year-old record of 189 not out against England – the crowd was deflated. Pin-drop silence descended in the stand after he reached a century and it became obvious that Saeed bhai had no intention of giving up. I think my own calls for runs – 'yes', 'no', 'wait', 'double' – were the only audible shouts in the field for most of his innings.

What a day! What an innings! Saeed Anwar at his finest. 194 from 146 balls. Twenty-two fours, 5 sixes – the highlight of the innings being dispatching Anil Kumble for 2, 2, 6, 6, 6 and 4. We set India a target of 328. But even Dravid's century – he too brought Tendulkar as his runner for no clear reason, and we objected,

successfully – couldn't help take India home. Pakistan won by 35 runs, Aaqib Javed being the pick of our bowlers, claiming five wickets. And for the first time in the history of the India–Pakistan rivalry – or so I was told by my seniors – about 50,000-odd Indian spectators gave the visiting Pakistan team a standing ovation. Truly, it was great cricket all around.

As a rival, as a team to visit on tour and as a country, India is unequalled when it comes to love and respect for cricketers. India's fandom is unique and different from that of the rest of the cricketing world. The country's affection for the game is unparalleled. Yes, their politics is dirty – remember how the pitches in Mumbai were dug up by the Shiv Sena? Their media plays dirty too, when they build hype by quoting things out of context. I think India's media has played a terrible role in distancing the two countries – strange, when people of both countries want peace. And more cricket.

After that first match in Chennai, I would go on to play four or five more games against India. There was one in 1998 – the Independence Cup final in Dhaka. Then in 2004, when I captained Pakistan 'A'. Then in 2005, when we won the Bangalore Test, under Inzi's leadership, and my famous Kanpur century (102 off 46, 10x4, 9x6). Then in 2007–8, under Shoaib Malik's captaincy, followed by the 2011 ICC World Cup and the T20s in 2012. What a journey it has been – to India and with India!

Over the years, Pakistan's tours to India got more complicated due to a host of issues, not all of them cricket-related. I've always believed, and I still do, that cricket is a great compromise between India and Pakistan. The game is a great stabilizer. It is the best way forward for normalization of relations between two estranged countries. Cricketers are the ambassadors, not just of the game, but of millions of people they represent and inspire.

With India, although our rivalry is the fiercest in the world, I believe that cricket is the best solution for peace. That's my single-line approach for normalizing Pakistan's relations with India: more cricket. Unfortunately, neither the Indian media nor the Indian government seem to agree. More on that later.

For now, I must admit something, even if it pains me to say this as a Pakistani. That initial psychological superiority we had established for years over the Indian team through the 1980s and maybe even the '90s has fizzled out. The magic of the famous Miandad six at Sharjah has worn off. For me, during the two decades that I played at the highest level, there's never been a better batting line-up in the modern game than the one India had during my time: Sachin, Dravid, Ganguly, Virender Sehwag, Yuvraj Singh. Now there's Virat Kohli.

For me, India was the most balanced, most dangerous side to bowl against. The rivalry is thus paramount. Period.

11

THREATS AND TREATS, INDIAN AND HOMEGROWN

1999. A military coup was about to hit Pakistan. Before that, the Kargil conflict would erupt between India and Pakistan. The stakes for peace were higher, we all knew. Both countries had conducted nuclear tests in 1998. I remember kids wearing 'Nuclear Powered Pakistani' T-shirts in Karachi. Nationalism was soaring in the subcontinent.

Still, when it started, 1999 bode well. Pakistan visited India for its first Test tour after thirteen years. That was most of my life, at that point. The gallant Wasim Akram, who would break Imran Khan's record of 362 Test wickets in the series, was captain of the side. Shehryar Khan, a gentleman-diplomat, was team manager. He would eventually become chairman of the Pakistan Cricket Board (PCB).

This was no ordinary tour – we all knew it. It didn't matter who would win. The 1999 tour was about history – the one that had been written and the one we were about to rewrite. A lot more than Test records were at stake. Unfortunately, prior to the tour, Indian nationalism turned into hyper nationalism. The right-wing Hindu supremacist group, the Shiv Sena, dug up the Delhi pitch at the Feroz Shah Kotla Stadium and damaged it badly. They attacked the offices of the Board of Control for Cricket in India (BCCI) in Mumbai. They even threatened to attack the Pakistan players. In short, they did all they could to disallow the series even before we set foot in India. (Apparently, the BCCI had to hire snake charmers to stay in the stands because the Shiv Sena had threatened to let loose cobras at the grounds.) There were protests in several cities – both for and against the series. This wasn't just any other tour – after all, Indian special forces commandos were to escort us everywhere in the country.

Sadly, the batting on that tour was below average. Just two players, India's Sadagoppan Ramesh and I, crossed the 200-run mark. The Delhi Test had to be moved to Chennai. We all came back to a terrible wicket in Delhi, though, and let 'Jumbo', Anil Kumble's new avatar, run us into the ground with his famous 10-wicket haul.

But neither Test went into the fifth day, so mediocre was the batting in both teams. Clearly, it was a series that belonged to the spinners. In Chennai, I got Sourav Ganguly's wicket – he was India's highest scorer of 54 in their first innings – and then went on to clean up the tail. Saqlain Mushtaq, by then one of my best friends, got a five-wicket haul in each innings of that series at an average of 20.15 and was awarded Man of the Series. On the Indian side, Kumble was the pick of their bowling and took advantage of an inconsistent home umpire in the first Test, but also brilliantly used the pitch – paved courtesy of the Shiv Sena – to crush us for a perfect 10 at the Feroz Shah Kotla Stadium in Delhi.

Kumble wrapped up the series with 21 wickets at an average of 14.85. What a guy! Even though I was the highest scorer for Pakistan in that second Test, I couldn't dominate him fully in that series.

For me, there were other lows on that tour – mostly within the Pakistan dressing room. During my innings of 141 at Chennai – off 191 balls, for over six hours of play, with 21 fours and 3 sixes where I went after Javagal Srinath and Co. – everybody in my team knew that Javed Miandad, the coach, didn't want me in the side.

The tussle had started even before the series kicked off. Miandad had developed a strong opinion against me, but Wasim Akram put his foot down, saying that if I didn't play, he wouldn't either. Of course, the skipper won and I tagged along. But the tension persisted and Miandad didn't relent. In fact, the day before I went to bat, Miandad didn't even give me any net practice. So I had to practise on a stringed ball, alone, away from my teammates. That was the cloud of angst and embarrassment under which I was playing my first Test against Pakistan's greatest rival. Imagine what I could have done with his support, considering what I managed to achieve without it.

In retrospect, I found Javed bhai very different from the hero we had grown up to cherish in the 1980s. Moreover, the conflict between the two of us was personal: about style, method and technique. He wanted me to play the way he played. He hated the way I batted. He didn't like my style, my technique or the lack of it. For me, batting was all about power plays and not exploiting gaps, but forcing your way into them. By that stage in my career, I knew I wasn't technically orthodox, but I had a thing going and it was working on the field as well as for the rest of the squad. But not for Javed bhai. He couldn't digest the way I played. I don't know why he took himself so seriously.

Our conflict had made things tough even before the tour had begun. His contrarian view about my place in the side added to a lot of team politics and anxiety on the tour. Instead of me, he wanted Asif Mujtaba in the side. It was only upon Wasim Akram's insistence and the chief selector Salahuddin Sallu's suggestion that I made the cut. The stage was set for a disaster. Javed bhai was relentless. And that's how the day before the Chennai match, he did something I consider highly unethical and unprofessional by not letting me bat at the nets. Bear in mind that I was the opener.

Of course, I played the match, scored that century and we even won the game by 12 runs. But Javed bhai's attitude towards me touched a new low. Before the post-match presentation ceremony, he pulled me aside and said, 'Listen, buddy, you'd better make sure you thank me in the presentation and interview. Tell them how I've groomed you and made you a good batsman. Understood?'

Yup. He actually said that. I couldn't believe it. It was just my second Test and I had seen the bitter reality of cricket politics already. That day I lost all my respect for Javed Miandad, supposedly one of the greats of the game but in reality, a small man.

I think I know what his problem is. Javed Miandad achieved great heights as a cricketer – bear in mind that my India obsession started with his six in Sharjah, one of the greatest moments the modern game has seen. But although he'd retired from the game, his sense of entitlement had not gone away. He wanted respect from anyone and everyone, at any cost. The situation is the same even today.

That's the thing about Javed Miandad. He lives in the past. His shadow is larger than himself. I feel it's the trait of a weak man. In his playing days, he earned himself a reputation, but retirement has brought out the worst in him. He even landed a political appointment – director general (DG) of the PCB. Nobody knows what he did as DG, though. In my opinion, no reforms, no new policies were implemented and nothing substantial was achieved during his tenure. Absolutely zilch, except six or seven years of a nice fat salary in his bank account.

The thing is, Javed bhai had – still has, maybe – a proximity complex. He would stick with those who performed. Those who were a bit inconsistent, like me, were dropped like a bad habit, perhaps because it was bad for his own reputation. Alas, he ruined one of my greatest cricket moments against my greatest rivals, by being, well, Javed Miandad. Being let down by your own, your elders, those you think you'd like to emulate, is the ultimate form of loss, especially in sport.

As for that series in India, we drew it 1–1. But cricket won. Big time. The crowds loved us. The press was all over us. It felt at the time that cricket in South Asia was back. However, for me, one of the gods of the game had fallen.

I have another sad tale, also from the field, about an episode surrounding another great innings. I was opening for Pakistan against India in the Sahara Cup at Toronto. Saeed Anwar, my fellow opener, didn't last long, and I was joined in the middle by the captain, Aamer Sohail.

I started with a six on the first ball and followed it up with two or three fours. The crowd went crazy. As the Indian bowler went to his captain to get some advice, Aamer came up to me. I approached him halfway on the track, for it looked like he wanted to discuss something. As soon as Aamer was near enough, he cussed at me, calling me a terrible name, and said: 'I know you've fixed this match with Wasim Akram. I know what you're up to, Afridi.'

My heart sank. This was in '97 or '98. I was young and just getting started in the game. I burst into tears in the middle of that pitch, with the game underway. But I recovered quickly – I went back to the crease, composed myself and tried to focus. Eventually, I succeeded; I scored a century.

Later, when I returned to the dressing room, Aamer, who had got out earlier than me, came up to the players' gallery and said, 'Stay on my side. Join me. I will connect you with the right people. I can help you run Pakistan cricket.' I just glared at him and walked away.

Later, I told Wasim bhai and Inzi bhai about the incident. They told me to keep the episode to myself and handle the situation gracefully and silently. Aamer Sohail was the captain, after all. I'm not sure where his insecurity came from, although I have a rough idea: it's about fame, or the lack of it, particularly in his case.

Remember, I was just a young lad, compared to these legends, these gods of cricket I was playing with. But right from the beginning of my career, I had something that was rare for a newbie like me: the pull.

Whenever I'd descend the elevator of any hotel in any city or country where we were on tour, the autograph hunters – folks these days just take selfies; the autograph, sadly, is a lost art form – who usually gathered around the senior, more well-known players, would simply abandon them and make a dash for me. It was after such moments that I began noticing that I'd inadvertently made some of my teammates insecure. My ears started picking up chatter too. I was 'the kid' who was 'just starting'. How could I get all 'the lift', it was asked. I heard it all, the chides and the uncomfortable silences, but I kept my head down and didn't make a big deal of it.

Greatness isn't an easy prospect. There are stars and then there are legends. I'm not talking about those who've been knighted. I'm talking about the gods of the game. It's a tough transition – there are plenty of stars in the Pakistan teams of yesteryears, but only a handful of legends.

Professional jealousy is understandable. If it forces you to up your game and motivates you to perform better on the field, it's healthy even. I encourage competitive behaviour. But when you mix jealousy with camaraderie and let it get in the way of teamwork, then it's all over. When you let your bad *niyat*, your ill intentions, get in the way of your job, which is to perform for your country, fans, family, honour – all for the love of cricket – then God makes things even tougher for you, and you spiral downwards.

There are haters everywhere. There's an entire movement online of trolls and hatemongers who exist on social media – or anti-social media, rather – who are anti-Afridi. I've heard that some of them actually get paid by some lobbies within the cricketing ecosystem to do what they do against me. Misbah-ul-Haq, one of our finest and most successful former Test captains, faces the same problem. Perhaps it's because we are both stars that we face these issues. I must confess that I do find the musings online rather interesting. But I don't worry about them too much.

Still, trolling is ugly. Super ugly. Organized trolling is a dark world by itself. But jealousy is a different beast altogether – it can undo the finest of men, even former world champions. If I don't get along with someone, I don't get along. Things are probably not meant to be pleasant at all times with that person. It was the same with Aamer Sohail when he hurt me with his comments. End of story.

Here's the truth. I will not always be *the* Shahid Afridi. I will not always be in a glitzy uniform or live a glamourous life. I will not always be 'one of the most dangerous players' of the game, strong of body and bank. Someone better, faster and stronger will come along. And then I will have to hang up my boots. I will err. I will fade away. These are my standards, weaknesses and strengths. These are the truths I must live with. These are the realities I am humbled by.

12

IGNOMINY IN ENGLAND

NOT A lot of men can claim to have experienced agony and ecstasy all in one go. I can. My first trip to England was for the 1999 World Cup and in the time we were such an exciting team that we made it all the way to the final at Lord's – the home of cricket – only to lose what will be remembered as the most one-sided World Cup final in history. Truly, the 1999 World Cup saw us at our best and, sadly, at our worst too.

Here's how we started. I opened against the West Indies, in Bristol, getting 11 in 19, and didn't bowl. We won, by 27 runs, in front of what felt like a home crowd. I also opened against Scotland in Chester-le-Street, getting 7 from 9. We won by almost a hundred runs. The Scots helped tick our scoreboard along too when they broke the record for extras conceded (48), maybe because they were hungover, or so their press claimed. Shoaib Akhtar wiped their top order clean. I barely bowled a couple of overs. There was too much movement off the pitch.

By our second week into the tournament, when we were up against Australia in Leeds, I was replaced by Wajahatullah

Wasti. Although we won that game by 10 runs, I felt that the inconsistency of Pakistani decision-making was beginning to show. A successful opening combination between Saeed Anwar and me was being played around with, for no odd reason. Keep in mind that in the 10 ODIs Saeed and I played for Pakistan before the 1999 World Cup, we opened together in the last nine matches (for the Coca-Cola Cup and the Pepsi Cup) to put up opening partnerships worth 577 runs for Pakistan, 297 of which were next to my name. So, in my humble opinion, as well as according to the math, there was no need to mess around with our opening combination. And yet, the Pakistani management was doing what it does best: defy logic.

Five days later, against New Zealand in Derby, I was back as opener with Saeed. I scored 17 in 22. Once again, it was Shoaib Akhtar who made a meal of their top order and we won by 62 runs.

One thing that sticks out from that World Cup – something I'd felt very weird about even then – was what happened before our next match, against Bangladesh. Everybody remembers that match – a non-Test playing side beat us down to pulp. I was caught for 2 off 4, trying to play a stupid shot. Still, I got my first wicket in the World Cup: the Bangladesh captain, Amin-ul-Islam – bowled for 15. The gloomy Pakistan batting figures can always be looked up, but what I went through that day cannot.

We had just got off the bus in Northampton and were heading to the dressing room. There was a huge crowd, mostly Asians, surrounding us. When I heard a bunch of guys shout: 'Pakistan is definitely losing today!' I couldn't locate who said it, but considering our form in the tournament till then, the comment didn't make any sense. I thought it was ridiculous. But those words stuck with me, both for the tone in which they were said, and especially in the light of the outcome of that game. We lost by 62 runs. It was that stray comment from a bystander which planted the seeds of doubt in my mind. Something seemed a bit odd.

Since 1998, there had been chatter that a match-fixing inquiry was required for Pakistan players. Now, after that World Cup game against Bangladesh, it became clear that something nasty was developing. I would find out later via reports in the press that our odds, according to legitimate bookies in the UK, were 33:1. However, there had been no reports about unusual betting in the UK. Instead, this was the first time I got to hear about the South Asian and Middle East bookie circuit – all illegal and underground, and a whole different world of betting.

The revelations were intense and disturbing. Here I was, just a lad in this great game, in this great team, fighting to win the greatest tournament of all. And here was this underworld, functioning and alive, beneath my very feet. It was unsettling. I was confused.

I remember during that tour, in the dressing room, we were all very driven and focused. We were hard on ourselves when we lost. We worked hard when we practised. The best of us used to scold ourselves when we underperformed. With the kind of dedication and sweat, blood and tears that would go into every game, it never occurred to me that some of us might have turned into sellouts, that too at the highest level of the sport.

What is even more strange is the way we bounced back in the tournament. At Nottingham, we met the other green giant, South Africa. Both sides were leading their respective World Cup groups. I was dropped, again – the inconsistency of the selectors was ridiculous at this stage – but was among the lucky ones to see one of the greatest matches in World Cup history. The match went down to the wire. Moin bhai's searing 63 destroyed Allan Donald's spell in the death overs and the game went the Proteas way on the last ball of the penultimate over when Saeed Anwar dropped Lance Klusener.

And then, it was time to take on India.

The battleground was Manchester, almost like a home turf for us. With the two nations' defence forces engaged in combat in Kargil, this wasn't any ordinary India–Pakistan face-off. We were aware of the stats: India had won all their previous games against us in World Cup history. Skipper Mohammad Azharuddin wanted to be part of the third such victory – the only Indian to do so at the time. He played that game like a man possessed, smashing a stellar 59 off 77 balls. Tendulkar was in his element. Dravid fired on all cylinders (I would catch him off Wasim bhai, but not before he put an incredible 61 runs on the board). As for our batting, Saeed bhai stood his ground till 36, but I went early, as did most of the top order. Inzi and Moin bhai put up a brave stand, but the pressure on us by then was so high, we had probably begun to worry about vandalism on the streets and flags burning back home. Though we would lose by 47 runs – and start developing a serious psychological problem about not chasing well against India – we would go into the final, and India would go home: out of the World Cup but still with a win against Pakistan hanging from their belts.

Then, a mirage was constructed. We cruised to the semis after shrugging off Zimbabwe – Saeed bhai got his first century in the tournament, Wajahat also finally clicked and Saqlain got a hat-trick to close the deal at The Oval. Batting at number seven, I was the third-highest scorer (37 off 29, 1x4, 2x6), finally understanding how to tackle a seaming English wicket. Playing me down the order at that position was working, although I wasn't comfortable batting in the slog overs. Those days, I still fancied myself as an opener.

But during the semi-final, against New Zealand, the day belonged to Saeed bhai and Wajahat – they made the biggest World Cup opening partnership of 194 – and Saeed bhai scored his second century in a row. Shoaib Akhtar, the Rawalpindi Express, who had already bowled the fastest ball of the tournament at 95 mph against South Africa, broke a Kiwi stump in each of his bowling spells in that match. We would win by nine wickets with 15 balls to spare. Despite all the doubts cast on the integrity of the side after our loss to Bangladesh, it felt like we were peaking at the right time.

I barely got any sleep the night before the final. Unlike the last time in a championship final involving the Aussies, there was no 'night out' either. There were a lot of young players with an unbelievable sense of pride in the team: Abdul Razzaq, Saqlain, Shoaib and I. Wasim bhai was leading us from the front. Never has a team like that been put together by Pakistan. It was a solid unit.

But in the aftermath of the Bangladesh match, there was doubt and controversy brewing. Personally, in a warm-up session before the final, I twisted my ankle while playing football. I was super stressed and up all night, icing the sprain, and eventually had to get a couple of injections to reduce the pain so that I could play the final. I wasn't in top form, but would still be the third highest scorer at 13 – which doesn't say much about the team, nor me.

As for the final – which was a disaster, with us all out for 132 in just 39 overs – we made the fatal mistake of batting first, especially given that the conditions were overcast and, as everyone knows, the ball moves around a lot in England on such mornings. Also, there was the Shane Warne factor to deal with as well. Warne – who scooped a record 20 wickets in the tournament – owned us that day. Our runs on the board didn't look defendable in any case. So, towards the end, our tail-enders just went after everything they could. The chase for the Aussies was easy and they wrapped up proceedings four and a half hours before time.

That match went down as the shortest final in World Cup history. It marked the beginning of the rise and rise of the Australians as the most ferocious ODI side in the world, and they would remain at the top for the next decade and a half. Of course, we were dejected by the outcome of the final – we have yet to make it to another World Cup final since that day – but there wasn't a lot of soul-searching in the Pakistan dressing room after the defeat. Wasim bhai told us all to chin up: we had made it to the final after a helluva run and had lost only to the finest, the Aussies. And that was that.

13
DECLINE

WITH THE new millennium came a wave of cricketing chaos. In early 2000, the Delhi police charged then South African skipper, Hansie Cronje, with match-fixing. Eventually, the ICC slapped a life ban on him. The same year, Pakistan's Saleem Malik and Ata-ur-Rahman also received life bans when faced with the same charges. By the end of the year, then Indian skipper, Mohammad Azharuddin, along with Ajay Jadeja, were also barred from playing the game. Once the 1999 World Cup ended, there was a global inquisition against the menace of corruption in cricket. The time had come to clean things up. Heads began to roll.

By the end of 2001, the cricketing world lost its greatest icon: Sir Donald Bradman, who died at the age of ninety-two. I regret not meeting him, even though I'd toured Australia. And even while the match-fixing saga was taking the subcontinent by storm, Australia were on a roll, the undisputed leaders of Test cricket, clocking 16 straight Test wins. Their professionalism was so good, it was scary.

Unfortunately, 2001 was also the year when terror, in its modern form, unleashed on Pakistan. First there were the 9/11 attacks in the

US, which shocked the world and then, soon after, shook our region, as the war in Afghanistan spilled over into Pakistan. In January 2002, Pakistan was forced to shift a Test series against the West Indies to Sharjah, as the Windies had turned down an invitation to visit Pakistan, citing security concerns. By summer that year, the Kiwis came over on tour – Inzi hit a brilliant 329 in Lahore – but once there was a bomb blast outside our hotel in Karachi, apparently targeting some French engineers, not us, our matches were called off. Worse still, Hansie Cronje, once among the game's most distinguished captains until the match-fixing controversy ended his career, died in a plane crash. Both in geopolitics and cricket, there was violence and volatility.

But amidst it all, I clearly remember that bombing in Karachi. We were at breakfast in the Pearl Continental, right across the street from the Sheraton. The lads were hanging out at different tables in small groups. The loners were at it by themselves. And then the ground shook. The noise from the explosion took out much of the windows. We heard screams and then pandemonium followed. Most people took cover under the tables or leapt into the kitchen area or the lobby on the far side.

I took a different approach. I exited the building and went out into the street, the PIDC Chowk, one of the busiest intersections of the city. I knew the area well. For years I had dropped by that spot for a late-night paan (and maybe a quick smoke to go with my betel leaf treat, though I'm not a regular smoker). It's a place where paan lovers from different parts of the city – the 'burgers' from Defence, the 'laundas' from Gulshan, the 'mailas' from Clifton – would congregate late in the night to enjoy the best 'saada khushboo' or 'tambaqoo wala' or the go-to 'meetha' in the city.

But that day, even before I could get to the street, I could smell the charred body parts of those killed and injured in the blast. I don't like to recall the exact details of what I saw, but I remember going to the policemen who had arrived on the scene and helping them out in clearing the area. Everybody was in shock and responding in their own ways. My response was to try and make sense of the surroundings and help restore whatever order that could be at the site of the bombing. I offered the cops water to drink and then departed from there once the ambulances arrived, so that the medics could do their job. It must not have been easy.

Later, I went to check up on our guests, the New Zealand team. They were scared and shaken up – we all were – and had assembled at the poolside, a safer spot since it was tucked inside a concrete enclave of the hotel. The Kiwis all flew back home soon after. What a terrible day for Pakistan, for the French (who were targeted) and for the game of cricket. As war and terror, and the war on terror, went global, it seemed that morning in Karachi that the cricket world was spiralling down too.

By 2002, the Pakistan team peaked again, and we overcame our World Cup final blues by beating Australia in a remarkably fought ODI series Down Under. There were a few of us young guns – Imran Nazir, Saqlain and I – in that team, but there were a few seniors who were hitting their own political snags as the year progressed. All that compounded into a far-from-ideal scenario in South Africa in 2003, where, under Waqar Younis's captaincy, we crashed out of the World Cup at the end of the group games stage itself. We didn't win anything of consequence. We lost our opening game against Australia, a match where we'd hoped to undo the loss at the 1999 World Cup final. But nothing special happened. Shoaib couldn't keep his mouth shut about Brett Lee. Nor could I for that matter – I was banned by the PCB for sledging against India (more on that in just a bit). Moreover, something had gone awfully wrong with our team's leadership. We were down, and then we were out.

Team sports can get complicated. But in order to function, every team must start with a basic tenet: a unit needs unity. And the Pakistan team didn't have much of it. There was a change in the chain of command and Waqar, the new man at the helm, was, unfortunately, a terrible captain. He couldn't hold us together. He couldn't fight off the politics inside the dressing room. I think he himself was responsible for much of it. There was a lot of ill will within the team at the time. It was a bad, bad time to be in the Pakistan side.

As usual, the press got it all wrong and made the divisions worse. There were reports about infighting within the team. An example that's often cited to substantiate such reports is the infamous scuffle between Inzamam and Younis Khan during a warm-up football session. The reports – that a rivalry was brewing between the two Test greats – were complete nonsense. Even I fought with Inzi at a football session around this period – hell, everybody must have fought with everybody during football, because that's what happens when cricketing gentlemen play this aggressive but beautiful game. It was part of the warm-up culture. That we were not getting along wasn't an accurate reflection of the state of the team.

The real story at the time was about our fall and was connected to the team leadership, or the lack of it. To me, there was no leadership. Waqar Younis is a lot of things, but he's no cricket captain. With Wasim bhai also available in the side, many of us – myself included – thought Waqar was a poor choice as captain. Neither could he control the team, nor could he inspire us. The rest is history and statistics (some of our most poor showings are stemmed in this time).

The whole matter is quite complicated, so maybe I should first elaborate a bit about the infighting in the team, which had reached a crescendo. You see, the captain's hat was the real crown in 2003. Consequently, there was a war between the two Ws – Wasim and Waqar. Naturally, there were two entrenched camps. Battle lines were drawn. Both Wasim and Waqar were fighting hard for the throne. Most of the team wanted Wasim to be the captain and he did lead us for a while. But then the chairman of the PCB, Lt Gen. Tauqir Zia, sided with Waqar – there was too much politics involved. It proved to be a really bad decision. The fact that Waqar was not captain material reflected clearly in Pakistan's dismal performance on the field.

So, in a way, there were three teams within the larger Pakistan unit: the older team (Rashid Latif, Inzamam, Saeed Anwar) on one side who were in Wasim's favour; the younger team (Azhar Mahmood, Mohammad Sami, Saqlain and I) who were looking for inspiration and had decided to keep out of the power politics that the seniors were involved in but wanted Wasim to lead; and then there was the Waqar group, which had Yousuf Youhana (later christened to Mohammad Yousuf) and the likes, although they eventually crossed over to Wasim's side. The problem, operationally, was a complicated one: Waqar was empowered, officially, but the team wasn't responding to him.

There was every reason to do well with the line-up that we had. The team had a fairly large coaching unit as well. On paper, we were a strong, solid unit. Hell, we had even trained well for South Africa. But we were not united. Simple. Team politics aside, some of the senior team members were, well, getting older. I felt we gave up too easily in several matches in that World Cup because of their flagging energy or the lack of it. Literally, it felt as if they threw in the towel. Against Australia, at five wickets down, we gave up. The same thing happened versus England and India. We didn't capitalize on our strong starts and this resulted in lacklustre finishes. Simply put, we were led by men who fought like children.

14
THE COMEBACK KING

I WAS dropped after the 2003 World Cup. I wasn't shocked. I hadn't done well with the bat in the tournament. Still, I made a comeback against India a year later. The comeback knock, 80 off 58 balls in a 138-run opening partnership off 19 overs with Yasir Hameed, will always be special.

That 2004 tour by India was a test of Pakistani hospitality and warmth. We all passed it and passed it well. Inzi and Sachin came together to shoot ads for fighting polio. The Indian team got a standing ovation in Karachi at the end of the first ODI, which they won off the last ball. Even I toned down my famous 'For India only' sledging. General Pervez Musharraf, president of Pakistan at the time, had the visiting side over for tea at his official residence. The Pakistan press loved the Indian squad. Moreover, India were on a winning spree – a 2–1 victory in the Test series and 3–2 result in the ODIs. It was a competitive tour by all accounts.

Just five years earlier, Pakistan and India had almost gone to war, and here we were, handing out commemorative T-shirts to the Indians. I even had them over at my house for dinner but committed an oversight only a Pashtun host can – there were no vegetarian options on the menu, just tons of meat everywhere. Thankfully, we reined in the crisis and managed to get some daal and palak ready for them in no time.

It was a joyous gathering, but a year earlier, things hadn't been as upbeat when I was dropped from the side. That was a rough time. Being dropped from the team after seeing so much early success and adulation wasn't easy. Nor was staying away from international cricket for twelve months. To be honest, I hadn't performed and deserved the boot. It was quite obvious after our dismal performance at the 2003 World Cup that some of us were not going to receive fresh contracts.

I wasn't worried though, because I knew I needed to improve. Therefore I didn't sit idle at home. I played whenever and wherever I could. It's the Pathan way – always be on the hunt for prey, big or small. Never wait around to scavenge for leftovers.

I went to South Africa and was lucky enough to be coached by Mickey Arthur at Kimberly. While I was there, I also bumped into the legendary Bob Woolmer. I would stay connected with Bob over that year and beyond. I remember he told me that he'd been following my career for a while and was surprised that I had been dropped from the team. Eventually, he was appointed coach of the Pakistan team – Javed Miandad got the boot after the home series against India, though Inzi bhai retained his captaincy – and I had an easy route back in, because Bob had seen me in action in South Africa and was gunning for me. We had bonded well there.

I was lucky but also aggressive about my goals. I'd known that performing well in South Africa, home to some of the fastest pitches in the world at the time, was key to making a comeback. I didn't go down the political route – *parchi*, as we call it – which a lot of other players take recourse to by getting a powerful political or administrative patron to push for them to be included in the team roster, sometimes for favours returned, sometimes for endorsements.

Instead, I did what I'm good at. I hit the ball around everywhere I could over those twelve months. I knew I'd be called back to the team. In hindsight, that comeback was easy.

Here's the thing: I like comebacks. Particularly in terms of what it does for you as a player, psychologically. Comebacks give you an objective, a point to prove, a target to hit. Aimless wandering isn't my thing. So, in a way, being dropped worked in my favour. I headed to other leagues – the SA league, or county cricket in the UK, or Australia whenever things went south in terms of form or performance. Then, on being given a chance to return, I'd do so with a bang, the same way I'd made my debut.

But I never let the pressure of being out of the loop affect my game or my approach to it. My comeback journey wasn't about getting runs on the board to make a place for myself in the team. It was about scoring runs and scoring them my way. Coaches tried to change my game; they failed. Eventually, it was Bob Woolmer who got it right. But in those early years, I was nervous about getting skinned by Miandad or the likes over a bad innings played my way. Honestly, I didn't care if I was or wasn't doing well, as long as I was doing things my way.

Anyway, after taking on India in 2004 at home, I was dropped again for the Asia Cup in Sri Lanka but picked for the tri-series against India and Australia in Holland (where I helped beat India), followed by the Champions Trophy, where I helped beat India again in the death overs with a cameo of 25. In those days, beating India was becoming fun again. While they had defeated us in the 2003 World Cup – I will never forget that blazing innings by Tendulkar at Centurion – maintaining their perfect 4-off-4 record against us in WC matches, Pakistan at the time still had a superior non-World Cup ODI win ratio by 2:1 over India.

Come 2005 and it was again time for the tour of tours for me – India. This would be Pakistan's first full outing to India in six years. The political context was different this time. After India's tour of Pakistan a year earlier, reciprocity was expected – both in terms of competitiveness and hospitality. Thankfully, the mood was peaceful. Our fans were allowed visas. People of both countries – and even the United Nations (UN) – appreciated the fact that Pakistan and India were using cricket as a confidence-building measure to normalize ties.

As for me, I was thankful for being back in the side: older and wiser than I'd been on my first visit to India. But I wasn't ready for what was about to happen on the ground. This time the political atmosphere was super-charged as my favourite leader at the time, President Musharraf, was also visiting the country. Personally, the tour was important for me as I'd just returned to the Test team. I was rested for the first Test in Mohali but I played the next two matches. In the second Test, at Kolkata, we cut off Sehwag at 81 and Tendulkar at 52. My modus operandi for batting was to open hard and hit their new-ball bowlers for the gallows. I had a strike rate of 119 in that game, with 29 from 21 in the first innings and 59 from 59 in the second. Too bad we lost by 195 runs.

In the Bangalore Test, which we won, thus levelling the series, I got three important wickets – Tendulkar, Ganguly and V.V.S. Laxman – in the second innings. I went through Ganguly's gate with a lot of movement, almost a metre in through a drive that he directed towards Bihar, not Bengal. He didn't leave the crease for a couple of minutes, thinking he'd been stumped, not bowled. It was fun watching him flummoxed. For Sachin, I kept it straight – we wore him out over a hundred balls before he reached double digits (to his credit, in that series he would beat Sunil Gavaskar's record for most Test runs, though). On the fourth afternoon, I hit 58 off 34, and almost beat Jacques Kallis's record of a Test 50 in 24 balls, just trailing by two balls. We went on to declare our innings with a lead of almost 400. Having been written off by even the Pakistan media, winning the game after trailing the series 1–0 was special. We won by 168 runs and the crowd, too, appreciated our performance. But here was a series that forced an Indian rethink too: Dravid's rise, Ganguly's fall – he was jeered by the Bangalore crowd – and cheers for Inzi, particularly at the presentation ceremony.

In the ODIs, it was classic India versus Pakistan. My strike rate was 173 across six matches. I got a century in Kanpur and took the pressure off our bowlers. We won the ODI series comprehensively (4–2) and President Musharraf even attended the last match in Delhi. Ganguly was hung up to dry by the press. Sehwag emerged as the mainstay pace-killer for India. Tendulkar kept obsessing over breaking Gavaskar's record of 35 centuries. We missed Shoaib Akhtar in that series; he was out with a hamstring problem.

We had high expectations from that tour. This applied to everyone but it particularly mattered in the case of my coach and mentor. The magic ingredient for me and my personal success was Bob Woolmer. His was the Midas touch. He gave me a lot of confidence, right from the time of our first meeting in South Africa to when I was dropped for a year. He told me that it was in India where a Pakistani player has to stand up to his ultimate test of greatness. And, most importantly, Bob was the first coach who told me to be myself.

15

AWKWARD AND OVAL

2006 WAS a year of conflict. I announced my retirement from Test cricket but soon came out of it and then announced it yet again. I was exhausted but also divided. Personally, I wanted to focus on limited-overs cricket but my friends and family wanted me to continue playing Tests. They had a point: some number-crunching will indicate that my Test career stats are more sound in comparison to my ODI career.

Frankly, I think my decision of leaving Test cricket was indeed a good one because I wasn't enjoying the format, personally. Yet, I didn't want to disappoint friends and family either – they have always played an important role in defining my career. Naturally, I was conflicted between choosing personal satisfaction over the expectations of loved ones.

Frankly, I was bored of Test cricket too. I couldn't play for five days. I couldn't play for five days if you paid me a million dollars per day. (On second thoughts, that's not such a bad offer and I may have reconsidered.) But seriously, Tests weren't my thing.

No *zabardasti*, boss, I said to myself. After all, I wasn't enjoying myself at the Test level. Before people blow my comment out of proportion, here's my official take: Test cricket is awesome. It's the ultimate form of cricket. It's what the spirit of cricket is based on. It's amazing, brilliant and brings out the best and the worst in players and their teams. But I've tested for Tests and have passed. I know that I'm done. Test cricket is not for me. You can hang on to your whites, thank you very much.

The travel was stressful too. Test series, especially those not at home, became a bit of a drag for me, for several reasons: the long tours, the non-stop travel, staying away from home and family for several weeks. Also, I'd entered the Test world a bit late, after 50-odd ODIs, by which time Test cricket was an add-on, not really what I was attuned to. Maybe if I'd debuted in Tests earlier, I'd have been mentally at peace with the format. (But if I start talking about how my career was mismanaged by the PCB, there will be hell to pay and another book altogether to publish.)

There's one more reason the year 2006 cannot be forgotten: the Pakistan–England Test match at The Oval. Test matches between the two countries have always been controversial, and here we were in the middle of a four-match series in the peak of English summer. We were optimistic going into the tour – England had won the Ashes in 2005 but were reeling from a captaincy crisis prior to our series. Pakistan, meanwhile, was in top form. We had managed to win four of our last eight Tests – England, India (both at home) and Sri Lanka (away) – and lost none.

Importantly, the Pakistan team had embraced spirituality in a big way as part of our mental preparation for each game. Inzi, our captain, had already established himself as a leader. He had a good working relationship with Bob Woolmer. The team's collective imagination was centred around Islam, which Inzi bhai had made the centrepiece of his style of leadership. Yousuf Youhana was now Mohammad Yousuf. I had let my beard grow too, just like

Inzi. We found unity in piety and prayed regularly. It reflected in our discipline, if not our performance. Some thought that it was a contentious path to take, but I think that just like some people push for a healthy work–life balance, we went through our own version of it – a cricket–spirituality balance. Sure, my other leaders in the past – Wasim, Waqar, Ramiz – had never been openly devout practitioners of the faith, but they were all good men. And here was Inzi, also a good man, in his own way.

Back to England, the usually scandal-prone summer tour was going rather well. Yousuf was the best batsman in our side, stylish and solid; Younis Khan was firing on all cylinders; Inzi bhai was getting consistent 50s. The rest of us were mediocre but still battle-ready. The only thing which was really hampering our squad was injuries. Our two strike bowlers, Shoaib Akhtar and Mohammad Asif, were out of the team due to various injuries. Neither Mohammad Sami nor Umar Gul nor Danish Kaneria were doing the job for us on the field.

We were trailing the four-match series 2–0. There had been some bad umpiring decisions in the third Test at Headingley already, and Inzi wasn't happy with both umpires officiating in the previous match: Darrel Hair and Billy Doctrove. Hair had a reputation for having an attitude problem towards Asian players. The PCB chairman at the time, Shehryar Khan, was considering putting in a formal request to the ICC to keep him away from all forthcoming Pakistan matches.

As for the contentious bit, everybody knows what happened. We walked away from that Test match thanks to an allegation by Hair – backed by Doctrove – that Pakistan's bowlers had tampered with the ball. As penalty, England was rewarded five runs.

We were stunned but continued playing. However, during the tea break, the senior players in the team backed Inzi and decided that they would not return to the field. To me, the umpires' behaviour was incomprehensible. But Inzi was affected on another level and was seething. The PCB officials couldn't convince him to return to the middle. Hair declared the match forfeited and awarded it to England. Eventually, we managed to overturn the decision at the ICC hearing, declaring the match as 'abandoned'. But later, the ICC reversed its own decision. A couple of months later, Hair was dishonoured and sacked anyway. He was a hateful racist. The end.

By the way, Hair stands disgraced now. In October 2017, he was caught stealing cash from a liquor store where he worked, in Australia.

In retrospect, there were a lot of alternative ways to deal with the situation on the ground. The Pakistan team could have walked off the field, like they do in Parliament, and returned. We could have talked to the match referee later and requested him to intervene. We could have gone to the press, even. But just leaving the game? I wouldn't have done it that way. I love and respect Inzi bhai and we all stood behind him that day as he was the captain. But I would have thought of a less confrontational way to save the match as well as our honour.

Yes, a Pathan just recommended non-confrontation. Take that and run with it.

16
THE BOY AND BOB

FOR TWO decades, I've been questioned about consistency. It's a subject that's been written about extensively. There have been debates about whether I was always immature at batting, whether I had the self-discipline required to stay at the crease for long.

Here's my side of the story. When I started playing in U-14 and U-16 cricket, I was a bowler. At the U-19 level, I batted at number seven or eight. Then, on my international debut, though I was inducted into the team as a bowler, God helped me set that batting record – the fastest century the game had seen at the time – which changed things. In fact, it changed everything.

Unfortunately, from thereon, I was slotted as a batsman, not a kid who bowls fast googlies and is useful with the bat too. I always was, and still remain, the latter. In hindsight, I know what really happened. That ODI century in Nairobi changed two things – perceptions and expectations. Moreover, it changed me – my focus shifted from bowling to batting. Simply put, it changed the direction of my career and my life. Right from the beginning, I had to respond to the surge in expectations, and that was tough.

Walking in to a stadium and hearing people screaming '*Chhakka!* (Sixer!)*' takes a toll on you, especially when you know you're simply a bowler who can bat on the trot. So, slowly, I tried to transition into a batsman. I was credited for a talent I didn't really possess. It was like being hired for a skill I wasn't exactly trained in. A kid who has always batted happily at number seven or eight, way down the order, is all of a sudden expected to open the innings against the bowling greats of the world. It was not easy – maybe it wasn't even the right thing to do, either – but I carried on, as that's what the job demanded.

Soon, I started seeing structural problems in my batting and reality hit home about how my overall performance was panning out. The biggest one, admittedly, was consistency. I couldn't be consistent. Not with my style and temperament. To give you an analogy of what was going wrong: if you know your weapons, you will agree that machine guns fire the fastest but get jammed the most, compared to other arms. Their rate of fire is both their strength and their weakness. Alas, I was the machine gun of cricket.

So, after a decade or so in international cricket, I started concentrating on two things only: bowling and limited-overs cricket. Till my retirement, I was still doing the same, by the way. I've come to appreciate that I can bat well once in a blue moon, but most of the time, I can't. I'm comfortable knowing that, even if my critics are not.

Today, I'm happy with myself knowing that I started off as a bowler, have come of age as a bowler, will always be a bowler, but can bat from time to time and even deliver some match-winning performances. A lot of people may think that's defeatism, but it isn't. I was always a bowler. I could open or go one down in a 10-over tape-ball match on the street, but really, in the proper format, I signed up to be slotted as a bowler. Too bad nobody was listening until much later. That's when Bob Woolmer came into my life and everything changed, once again.

Just to be sure, I'm not saying I got pushed into batting. My maiden ODI ton was nothing short of a miracle. It sure felt like one, too. But after that game, with the increased attention and overnight stardom, there also came the burden of unrealistic expectations everywhere I went.

People used to say it all the time, and some of them still do: 'Wow! We love you, Afridi; we love your sixes; we love your shots; hit a six today.' It was almost as if I couldn't hit anything but sixes, as if I couldn't play the game any other way. That is what people began to expect from my batting. And I let it all get to me.

Maybe it was because I was young and naïve that all their comments went to my head. My excuse to myself was simple – this aggressive style of batting, this brutal power hitting, is what people like about me; this is all they expect from me. So, the pressure to play an innings filled with blinding hard knocks only mounted. It never relented, at least not in the early days.

There were pressures from elsewhere too. My coaches – there have been so many – always advised me to change my natural game. They wanted me to bat like them, to play the way they did in their playing days. That was unfair. It is this sort of coaching that was a disaster for me, personally. Had they accepted my innate style, my God-given talent, polished what I could do naturally with the bat and not stopped me from playing instinctive, aggressive shots, I believe I would have significantly improved my batting average. Instead, they tried to make me someone I was not.

So, yes, in those early years in the national side, I was under a lot of pressure – there were expectations from the press, the dressing-room, crowds egging me on as I walked to the crease, the coaches holding me back from playing the way I like to play … I think I became severely conflicted. On the one hand, there were the fans and their expectations; there were the people who believed in me and who made me believe that I had changed the game. On the other were these constrictive, conservative coaches who didn't see what I *could* do but only saw what I *should* do.

I didn't know how to play amidst such confusion. I honestly believe that I was damaged by all that pressure and didn't handle it well at all. At times, my performances became so dismal, I felt like a child who had been given a bat and sent in to face the world's greatest bowlers. For several years, I lost my focus and even my core strength: my confidence.

I'm not pinning all the blame on my coaches but had they given me some confidence, said, 'Hey, you bat the way you want ... do your thing, I support you', I would have excelled a great deal. But after all these years, I can safely say that the only coach who gave me that kind of support was Bob Woolmer.

I challenge anyone: go and check my batting stats during Bob's stint as Pakistan coach. You will notice that my performances were better in every aspect. That's because Bob never stopped me. In fact, he encouraged me to play my natural game. He never got in my way during regular matches, and before any big, crucial games, he'd tell me, 'Go play the way you want to play. Just destroy the other team and don't leave anything unsettled for tomorrow. No regrets.' Those were the only words I needed to hear. It was due to his coaching that I found my confidence, my groove again. My killer instinct with the blade returned somewhat.

But Bob was an outlier and, God bless his soul, we still miss him. As for the rest – coaches I've worked with, coaches I've never been able to work with – even though I'm very straightforward, I kept tolerating the wrong treatment from many of them only because I respected their position, if not them.

I must emphasize here that I don't think a good player necessarily makes for a good coach. Coaching is studied. There's a science to it. It's technical in nature and based on instruction and construction. At the international level, where skill sets are already so good, coaching is more about mental conditioning and keeping a player relaxed and confident, not just super fit and well-trained. So, to be a good coach, one needs to study and learn how to be one. You can't just show up and start coaching because you played for some major team and have several accolades to your name.

I may be wrong here but coaches also need to unlearn a lot of things to make sure that the team members, who may be a new generation of players, can play the game under optimal guidance. In any given situation, there is no formula for running a team or a unit. A father with six children cannot treat them all the same way. Every child has their own thing going on; some of them learn from love, and some of them learn from the stick. A good coach is like a good father – he has to treat his children according to the way they respond to change.

I remember Bob did something no other coach did for me or for the teams I played in. He made us perform based on our natural, organic potential. Being a cricketer is one thing. Being a coach is another. Being a selector is yet another. Bob had learnt the art of being a coach. He knew about my personality, what I was capable of. He knew how to get me going. Similarly, he knew how to motivate my teammates. Coaching at the international level is not about hand-holding or pampering or step-by-step guidance. I wasn't some kid fresh out of A-Levels. Whenever I was under pressure, Bob would remind me of who I really was and convince me that what I had done in the past, I was capable of repeating again.

Now that I think about it, I really wish Bob had been my coach from the beginning and given me the confidence to let me play my game. My performances could have been more consistent over the years. I may have become a much different player, maybe a different man altogether. But we lost him too soon.

With his passing during the 2007 World Cup, I went through the most challenging phase of my career. Being banned for the first couple of games – why on earth! – was bad enough. The loss to the West Indies in the opener and then to Ireland on St Patrick's Day – all causing our early exit from the tournament – was bad enough. And then, just like that, the night of the Ireland game, he was gone.

I have ghastly memories of the days that followed. The cops. The press. The hatred. The pressure. The speculation about his death being murder by strangulation and/or poisoning by some sort of underworld betting mafia. The connections drawn to us, wrongly, of course. In my twenty years as a cricketer, it was the toughest time for us as a team. We couldn't even sleep. I remember, we all had single rooms but none of us felt like sleeping alone. We were scared. The night of Bob's death, we all teamed up in twos and threes in our rooms to feel safe. Even the skipper, Inzi, shared a room, with Mushtaq Ahmed, then part of the coaching staff. Think about that – a strong, solid man like Inzamam-ul-Haq, reduced to the fear of being alone. I don't think I ever saw him face a tougher time as a captain. It depresses me even to think about it today. We never really got over it. I know I didn't. Yes, things got better when we got home. But I hated it. All of it.

After Bob's demise, the PCB announced a slew of measures to restructure the team. It formed a bunch of committees. There was a call for a new era and a rebuilding of the team. Inzi lost his captaincy. Shoaib Malik was appointed the new captain, a decision that came with its own bunch of problems.

At twenty-five, Shoaib wasn't fit to lead Pakistan. Conceptually, it was a good decision, but the PCB messed up in several ways. First, they got me involved, asking me if I wanted to be vice-captain. That post eventually went to Salman Butt anyway, and as the records show, the PCB's disregard for seniority would chafe many of us. Second, Malik's captaincy made the fissures within the team even wider as 'groupism' and dressing-room politics became rampant. The 'senior-versus-junior' tussle that began in 2002–3 eventually went over the top. As a result, we didn't end up winning any major tournaments. Worse was the combination of leadership: Malik was barely an acceptable captain to the side, while Butt wasn't tolerable at all. To be sure, most of us couldn't accept him as vice-captain; I certainly did not. Moreover, Butt's subsequent promotion and tenure as captain was an infamous one. (More on that in the pages to come.)

And then came the bounce back. Or an attempt at one.

After Bob's demise, our next ODI series was in Abu Dhabi against Sri Lanka in May 2007. It was a case in point of Pakistan's sheer grit against all odds.

In the first ODI game, chasing 236, we were struggling at 137 for 5. We still needed 99 runs, with 18 overs to go. There was enough time. But there weren't enough men.

I came in at number seven and Kamran Akmal was at the other end. Thanks to our partnership, we were home in 11 overs. I got 73 from just 34 (8x4, 4x6) and was especially kind to Malinga Bandara, sending him reeling for 32 runs from his last over. What helped was that we were playing in Abu Dhabi; it almost felt like playing at home. The crowd is made up of a majority of Pakistan supporters, mostly Pathans. I got four straight sixes in. Bob Woolmer was gone but his words were still with me – 'Always be yourself' – and my A-game was back on.

The cricket was interesting – a hallmark of Pakistan's version of the game. We were in a corner and had to make a comeback. We were under pressure. We were angry; hell, I was seething. The two-match ban didn't help. But my knock did. All of what was happening around us was so negative and unpromising. So yeah, in that lone victory against the Lankans, we bounced back, mentally at least.

The tournament would continue on the same pace. We sealed that first match and then I helped Shoaib captain the side to victory through the second game – we were defending 313 on board – as I picked up three wickets.

Alas, those two victories were just a false start in a series of failures. In the subsequent months, we would not do very well under Shoaib's leadership. His lack of experience was his shortcoming. He was, after all, just a kid. Years later – older and wiser – he would shun the captaincy as he himself would realize that he's not skipper material. A helluva cricketer, yes, but no leader. But during that crucial time, it was an unfair to both him and the team to have him appointed as captain. I believe he wasn't ready. And in the wake of Bob's death, during that turbulent, sensitive time, that decision cost us doubly.

17

SKIPPER, VICTIM, SOLDIER, TERROR

THEY SAY there's a lot of politics in the Pakistan cricket team. They are probably right.

A captain is like a tower. He has to rise above the rest and provide a sense of direction. To achieve that, he has to let go of his personal issues. More than anything, he has to let go of the past, as everybody depends on him for the future.

Look at Imran Khan. We all know that he didn't personally like a lot of players who played under him. We all know he had an abrasive, confrontational, take-no-prisoners style of leadership. But he never got personal. Regardless of his own feelings about any of his players, he got the best out of them, professionally. By the way, they say that Khan, now prime minister of Pakistan, runs his cabinet the same way. More on that when I talk about his 'Naya Pakistan'.

When Shoaib Malik took charge, he couldn't replicate Imran's magnetism. He couldn't rise above the petty politics of the dressing room that had taken over during the Wasim–Waqar spat and never really stopped. His biggest problem was – and maybe it still remains to this day – that he was *kaan ka kaccha*, someone who believes everything he hears. He was prone to taking bad advice from bad people. In my opinion, he wasn't ready for the role.

I'm no diplomat, though, and I let my frustration slip out more than once about Shoaib's captaincy, and especially Butt's vice-captaincy – both bad moves from the PCB. I remember, at a preparatory camp for the 2007 World T20, there was an incident on the team bus that set the tone on where I stood on the matter.

Here's what happened: the players were in the bus, on their way to the hotel. I climbed on board and took my usual seat. Talat Ali, a very opinionated team manager at the time, told me rather rudely to get up and leave my seat for Salman Butt, the newly appointed vice-captain. I didn't budge from my seat and told Ali to take a walk. This was no way to treat the senior members of the team, I thought. In Pakistan, it's part of our culture to respect elders and seniors. Just because the team was being led by a junior, arbitrarily in charge because of an arbitrary decision by a largely arbitrary board, didn't mean that our culture of respect and achievement should not be adhered to. The leadership choices made had been bad decisions and I'd already been pretty vocal about it. It was bad enough that senior members of the team were looped out of important conversations and decisions – and worse that we were not even being allowed to take our usual seats on the damn bus.

It's simple. I'm no soldier. I won't just take orders and go to war. I will not say 'Yes, sir'. Not to just anyone. But I am a warrior. I will fight till the end for anybody who inspires me. And Shoaib Malik and Salman Butt were not inspiring.

With these complex equations and tensions within the team, we went to the World T20 with Shoaib as a contested captain. We lost to India in the final with that infamous scoop by Misbah-ul-Haq in the last over. It was a scoop that should have been a leg glance. Or a flick. Or even a paddle or sweep. But forget Misbah's shot selection.

We all fought hard in that championship, though. I was Player of the Tournament. Tensions within the team prevailed. Keep in mind that around this time, although dressing-room politics were peaking, we were still performing.

Only Pakistan is capable of undergoing both – excellence on the field and deterioration in the dressing room. Worse, players were leaking information to the press about what was going on within the rank and file. Some of them were even being blackmailed by reporters to talk about each other and spill the beans about the fissures within the unit. The good thing was that many of those tensions remained behind closed doors, despite the dog-eat-dog politics of the Shoaib Malik era. However, statistically, it was clear that Shoaib's captaincy wasn't doing wonders for Pakistan cricket.

The India series in November–December 2007 is a case in point. It's a tour I'd rather forget. Simply put, Shoaib was just not inspiring enough. Eventually, he would be left out of the side due to an injury; an unprepared Younis Khan would take over the reins for the rest of the series. By 2008, the fuel had completely run out of Shoaib's captaincy. Only second-tier teams like Zimbabwe or Bangladesh were coming to tour Pakistan, anyway.

Then, in January 2009, Younis bhai – who had earlier been offered the captaincy position twice and he had turned it down – accepted an offer to become skipper of the side. It was heralded as a good decision, a long time coming. One had hoped that Pakistan cricket would rise from there. However, about a month later, tragedy struck when the bus carrying the touring Lankan side was attacked by armed gunmen in Lahore. The match was abandoned, declared drawn. And with that, Pakistan cricket hit rock bottom.

I will never forget that terrible day – the attack on 3 March 2009. I was in Muzaffarabad – the capital of the Pakistan-administered territory of Kashmir – with Moin Khan, busy with flood-relief work and helping out with the inauguration of a hospital. It's ironic that I heard about the terror attack when I was in one of the most conflicted and militarized regions in the world. Moin and I couldn't believe what we'd heard. Immediately, we feared the worst, that we'd lost our teammates and colleagues, and worried about what would now happen to Pakistan and Pakistan cricket.

Politically speaking, the attack was inevitable, really. After the 9/11 terror attacks in the US, Pakistan had chosen to fight the war against terror as a partner of the North Atlantic Treaty Organization (NATO). But it was a war that wasn't ours to begin with. Yes, we had chosen to side with the Americans, but I'm not sure if we were prepared for the implications of teaming up with them.

Eventually, as the war came home – spilling over what was being called the 'AfPak Border' into mainland Pakistan – it became our struggle. But what happened to the Lankan team that afternoon in Lahore made it pretty clear to Moin bhai and me that there would not be much international cricket in Pakistan, not anytime soon. Indeed, Pakistan was declared unsafe for several years. But the Lahore attack, in our cultural capital in the heartland of Punjab, on our treasured tradition of cricket, really broke us all down.

Some folks might disagree, but I don't think any other nation has given up more to fight terror than Pakistan. In the last couple of decades, no nation has spent more blood and money in this fight than Pakistan. Over 80,000 casualties sustained. Over 130 billion dollars spent. But what the official numbers won't tell you is the toll on our national polity and psyche. Frankly, we've done a lot more than our fair share. Pakistan has done most of the heavy lifting to fight this ongoing war and it continues to do so.

Today, when I look back, I can't believe that amidst all that isolation which followed the Lankan attack, Pakistan cricket has managed to do rather well despite not playing at home for almost a decade. The team's resilience was evident soon after the attack.

Less than two months after Lahore, we went to Dubai to play Australia. Personally, I did well in the series – some useful cameos down the order along with one six-wicket haul. We would lose the series, though. Still, delivering individually against the Aussies is always good for one's confidence. But in the wake of Lahore, even though we lost the series, this was confidence we really needed. We would use that momentum soon after, in June that year, to play the World T20 in England and win the final comprehensively at Lord's. A few months earlier, Pakistan had felt deeply ashamed, letting harm come to its guests, the Lankans. But on the day of that final, we stood tall and proud at Lord's, this time beating the Lankans in a game, fair and square.

Believe it or not, when the tournament began, the Pakistan team was written off and not even considered a contender for the title. After the attacks in Lahore, it was clear that no cricket-playing side would express interest in touring Pakistan. Moreover, we had recently lost to the Aussies. In the early stages of the championship, we didn't do much to beat this impression and lost to England and Sri Lanka in the group stages.

But after taking a beating in the initial round, there was no looking back. Some of the things that transpired for Pakistan had to do with changes I underwent myself.

Personally, I tried to be responsible. I don't know where the motivation came from but I truly wanted things to change. Moreover, everybody had had enough of Afridi the Terrible. Afridi the Undependable. Afridi the Bludgeoner. Afridi the Hitter or Misser.

Something had to change.

The semi-final against the Proteas was an indication of what I was trying to do to transform; I didn't hit even a single six in 45 balls, but I still reached the half-century mark. I took on additional responsibility and played a very 'un-Afridi'-like innings (I'd had a 50s' drought for years). And throughout the tournament, I delivered with the ball as well – I hit the stumps seven times while bowling and had an economy rate of under six.

You could say that anger and being cornered on the world stage helped me come back to form. Also, the timing was right. The mental approach was the correct one. The attack on the Lankan team had given us the impetus to fix things. Winning the World T20 was a benchmark we wanted to set. Not united by much as a unit, this time, after the Lahore attack, we all had a point to prove. We made a slow start but caught on after the New Zealand match, thanks to Umar Gul's magical spell and my crazy catch in that semi-final (running backwards at what felt like 100 mph, I felt like the world was ours to conquer).

And then I asked our captain, Younis Khan, if I could bat up the order.

I did so not for mere victory. I had a larger goal: I wanted to take more responsibility. It was important to comprehensively clinch the semi-final against South Africa – we knew that we had a chance against them; we knew that in crucial knock-out games they had earned a reputation of being 'chokers'. That's why I asked to bat up the order: to change our approach, our strategy, and to create unexpected pressure on their bowlers. That's why that particular match will always go down as one where I didn't play like myself. We knew that the semi-final was more important than the final. Once we advanced from the semis, we were confident that that momentum would allow us to win the final. So it was our motivation and determination to make things right and it helped our cause.

I liked those early days of Younis Khan's captaincy. He is a democrat. He dealt with all players equally – that was his strength and wisdom. Although not a natural at leading a side, just like he wasn't a naturally gifted cricketer, he had the ability to handle us according to our individual sensitivities and whims. As a result, the mood in the Pakistan dressing room in those days became rather congenial. The World T20 victory helped, with us flattening the Lankans and lifting the trophy so soon after we had experienced the trauma of the Lahore attack.

But the gloomy legacy of the Pakistan team – much like the country it represents – is its inability to fight its inner battles.

Soon after that tournament, Younis bhai's captaincy unravelled and things really started disintegrating. The era of politics and infighting that followed eventually led to one of the darkest periods in Pakistan cricket.

18
THE STRAIN OF COMMAND

I WON'T name him, but one of the seniors in the team at the time – a great batsman in his own right – was majorly responsible for the breakdown of stability and goodwill within the Pakistan team. It saddens me to write this because he was one of the finest batsmen in those years.

A couple of months after the World T20, during the ICC Champions Trophy in South Africa in September 2009, this batsman essentially attempted a coup: he called a team meeting of the major players sans the captain, Younis Khan (Ijaz Butt was the PCB chairman and I was vice-captain at the time). In this 'midnight conference', he claimed to speak for all players when he announced that he was not satisfied and motivated under Younis Khan's captaincy. That was that – he had declared an all-out rebellion, bang in the middle of a major tournament.

To be sure, in those days, there were occasions when Younis used to mess things up for himself and everyone else by losing his temper. I don't mean to stereotype, but he is a fellow Pashtun, after all, and is prone to flare-ups. Aggression is part of our leadership style. Still, that didn't call for a full-blown rebellion against a very well-qualified captain and one of the game's finest batsmen. But that's exactly what the dissident batsman tried to do and – rightly or wrongly – he had enough followers to disrupt our performance. Personally, I felt he was overreacting and the idea of a rebellion was a bit extreme.

When the dissident told me his plan to marshal the players and inform Ijaz Butt that nobody wanted to play under Younis – all this in the middle of a tournament – I tried to convince him otherwise. First, I said that it was unfair of him to lobby other players into feeling as dissatisfied as him, especially the younger players. Second, I advised him to take the matter directly to Younis Khan and tell him, man to man, what his concerns were. I even offered to broker peace between them. The dissident refused. Moreover, Shoaib Malik (the former captain), Naved-ul-Hasan and Saeed Ajmal also endorsed his plan. He had a lot of firepower behind him.

I felt isolated. As vice-captain, with the Champions Trophy going on, I wanted the matter to be resolved and not to implode further. So I consulted Yawar Saeed, the team manager, and asked him to set up an appointment for the team to meet with Ijaz Butt. It took a while to get dates and in the meantime, the tournament continued. Eventually, when Butt sat us down, all the players opened up about what their problems were with Younis.

When it was my turn to speak, I said that the issues outlined could be sorted out – there was nothing that a team couldn't resolve sitting across a table. I also recommended that Younis be called in and allowed to proactively participate in solving the problems so that we, as a team, could emerge from this situation together – not at anybody's expense.

That was the end of the meeting. Later, I approached Ijaz Butt in private and reiterated that Younis was a great captain and that he should be allowed to retain his captaincy. I emphasized that the problems the boys had should be taken to him in a transparent fashion to avoid a similar situation in the future.

The repercussions of that meeting were as expected. The atmosphere in the dressing room became quite tense and uncomfortable. Later, when Younis was eventually sacked as captain – and we were knocked out of the Champions Trophy – I was declared captain of the side, temporarily. Since I already knew everybody's mindset, I was aware of how ugly the game of team politics could get, and proceeded with caution. This was not the ideal time to wear the captain's hat. Eventually, the dissident batsman was made captain for an overseas tour. When Pakistan didn't win a single game on that tour, the same things – conspiracy and controversy – hit him too. The moral of the story is simple: if you dig a hole for others, make sure you don't fall into it yourself. Sadly, that's what happened to our rebel.

The bottom line is a stark one: the atmosphere in the dressing room in the years leading up to the 2010 spot-fixing scandal was really toxic. In my opinion, things began going downhill the day the PCB chairman at the time, Dr Nasim Ashraf, breached all traditions of seniority and experience and made Shoaib Malik the captain and Salman Butt the vice-captain. That single move tore the team apart and it took several years for Pakistan cricket to recover from it.

Here's the thing: sometimes, it's natural instinct that's the enemy. It's normal to start looking for others to blame when you lose. And, when you win, it's normal to take all the credit for yourself. That's broadly what happened to the Pakistan team in those dark days of politics and scandal. We should have taken ownership of not only our wins, but also our defeats. Sadly, we couldn't fight our natural instinct of selfishness.

By the time I was appointed captain in 2009 – first, for all T20 internationals and eventually, for ODIs – I'd learnt a few lessons the hard way, so I developed a radical approach towards my job.

Delivering a standout performance on the field was not my priority
– discipline was. I made it very clear to everyone that if I saw any
politics in the dressing room, be it from someone who'd scored a
century or from a match-winner, I would get him kicked out of
the team. That was my code: discipline, minus the politics. This
approach was from the Imran Khan school of thought. That was also
the pact Waqar Younis, the new coach, and I had made. I'm glad
that since that time, till today, we've never had a better atmosphere
in the dressing room. After my innings as captain, Misbah-ul-Haq
took charge of the dressing room in similar fashion and conducted
proceedings wonderfully without any politics or infighting.

I hate politics. It is something we can do away with in every field
and organization in Pakistan. We ooze politics and palace intrigues.
The politics I saw in those difficult years in the team was the worst
kind, driven by ego and self-aggrandizement. Some players had
begun fancying themselves as the new Imran Khans, thinking that
the whole team clicked on their efforts alone. They thought they
were born leaders, but were far from it.

A true leader always takes his team along on his journey. A true
leader is one who, even in a crisis, stands up first and comes forward
before the others are held accountable and assures the team: 'I'm
here, I'll take care of everything.' That's what makes him good. He is
the guy who steps up to bat, to bowl and to face the fire.

As skipper or even otherwise, a habit that I'm proud of is that I
spent more time with my juniors than my seniors. With the latter,
I had a different approach. The night before a big game, I used to
take my seniors out for dinner, ask them for advice, understand their
approach, gain their confidence and just generally be on the same
page in terms of strategy and tactics. With the juniors, however,
I used to hit the beach, play football, head out for a meal or plan
a relaxed evening. That was how my leaders, greats like Wasim
Akram, had groomed me. Sadly, that wasn't how some of these other
'wannabe Imran Khans' worked. If you want to be a dictator, you

should command an army, not a cricket team. That's my advice to any aspiring cricket captain.

My intention of being close to the juniors was to stay aware of their issues and understand what was on their mind. It helped me know them intimately and have a better pulse on the team. This way, I could help them, even if the issues they faced were to be tabled in front of the PCB. Being close to the guys – that was my style. Today, by the grace of God, I can seriously challenge anyone: ask any member of the Pakistan team who has played with me over the last few years and they will tell you that their best times have been under my captaincy. Our winning statistics may be a different story altogether – I'm talking about honesty, discipline and team morale.

There have been some who have criticized me for having a 'relaxed attitude' towards the boys when leading them. Fair enough – I never stopped any of them from partying and enjoying themselves. They're young sportsmen, after all. I understand their point of view and their expectations. I would even consider hanging out with them, if possible. My only demand from the boys was this: even if you give me 10 per cent discipline off the field it's acceptable. But give me 110 per cent on the ground, where it matters most. Give me all the sweat and blood that you can produce when you're on the field. Give me that and you can do whatever you please before or after the match. The boys, during my brief tenure as captain, were reasonably happy with this arrangement and they delivered too.

19

CAPTAINCY AND CHAOS

THE ATTACK on the Sri Lankan team bus in Lahore had some influence on our winning the 2009 World T20. Strike that. It had *everything* to do with our win.

As a team, we were already under pressure in the tournament, having lost to England and the Lankans in the group stages itself.

Slowly, there was a revival of sorts. First, individual performances started to peak. For example, Umar Gul's spell against New Zealand (3–0–6–5) was wonderful. In the same match, I took a crazy running catch to get Scott Styris out when he was looking dangerous at 22, all set to take the Kiwis home. I still remember that catch – my God, running towards the long-on boundary. That dismissal was the turnaround moment for Pakistan – we all knew it. That moment was the game changer.

The surge in performances continued. Against South Africa, the best match of the series, I played an out-of-character 50. Before that game, I had been written off by most critics. By the time it was halfway, I was blowing flying kisses to Jacques Kallis after every pull shot I got off his bowling. The secret, for me, was batting up the order, at number three. I remember, after that New Zealand game, I'd gone to Younis and just flat out asked him to promote me up the order. He didn't cross-examine my request. I think my tone made it very clear to him what I wanted to do. It was like a warriors' pact: we were all in the mood to take risks. We were all feeling, playing, breathing a bit differently. So when I smashed Kallis all around and then dispatched Johan Botha for four successive boundaries, my captain and I knew exactly what I was up to. When it came to bowling, I dismissed Herschelle Gibbs and AB de Villiers, bowling them through their gate.

You see, for the first time in a long time, I was playing with abandon. I was free emotionally. I remember telling Indian commentator Harsha Bhogle that I wasn't taking pressure anymore. Pakistan had hit rock bottom. International cricket had literally been gunned out of our country. Thus, in the last two matches of the tournament, I just felt different. I was batting with a whole different mindset. After years, I was talking to myself, out there in the middle. I knew this was a chance to redeem Pakistan. I had worked hard. It all paid off when we clinched the championship.

In the final, too, I was an innings builder, not a butcher of the opposition's attack. I didn't score a boundary till I was at 17 from 19 balls. That's when I took Muralitharan out for a six and a four, consecutively, and slowed down again. I turned on the heat again in the 18th over. I wanted the crown for Pakistan, especially because of what had happened back home, just a few months earlier, in Lahore. But I was in no rush to get it.

There itself I was experiencing a metamorphosis at a personal level. I wanted to win and win more.

Younis Khan would retire from T20 internationals that day. He would dedicate our victory to the memory of Bob Woolmer. He would implore the world to visit Pakistan to play cricket. That day, at Lord's, we were kings. And we deserved the crown more than anyone else.

Then, of course, came scandal – typical of Pakistan. The whitewash in the Australia tour. Yousuf and Younis were banned. Even I was banned for biting the ball – something I'd done out of sheer desperation. I'm sorry for it and will always regret it. I did it so that we could win. I was wrong.

But I need to talk more about what was happening beyond stupid mistakes. This was a time for reckoning. I was going to become captain.

Honestly, it's all about *niyat*, intentions. I am crystal clear about leadership starting with good *niyat*. Without it, no help comes your way from God, or from others. One must have a clear and clean *niyat* for everyone. It's an approach I reserve even for adversaries, like Yousuf – despite our differences, I wanted him in my squad. In the same manner, I put behind bad memories with some other guys too. I gave opportunities to the younger members of the team. Some of them took advantage of it and did well. Some did not and to this day they are struggling.

I spent a lot of time building confidence amongst the younger guys. It was important for me to know what they were thinking, what their fears were, how they wanted to approach our game. Sometimes I broke protocol and took them out shopping, eating and even partying. I was in no mood to lose a game on the field, or my team's confidence in me. I didn't want to give up my captaincy for the sake of protocol and decorum. There was no obligation to maintain a certain distance with me. I wanted them to tell me what was on their mind, if they wanted to bat at another position, if they were in trouble with the PCB or the management.

As captain, my first tour was to Sri Lanka for the 2010 Asia Cup. I hit two centuries and was Player of the Tournament. The team lost, but people started noticing something – that I had brought back the team's fighting spirit; that I was a different man as captain;

that I was bringing the team back on the world stage as a match-winning side.

I took risks too. I promoted myself up the order. I took my game by the horns. I decided to step up as a batsman. As captain, I had a point to prove in the Asia Cup.

We almost clinched the first match against India. I got a 32 from 25, but our finest bowling attack in a decade – Shoaib Akhtar, Abdul Razzaq, Mohammad Amir, Saeed Ajmal, Shoaib Malik and I – let the game slip on the second-last ball, letting Harbhajan Singh smash Amir for a six over mid-wicket.

I tried to redeem us in the match against Sri Lanka, coming in at 32/4 while chasing 242, and smashing 109 from 76. Muralitharan paid dearly that day, conceding 71 in his 10 overs, most of them to me – I hit him for five sixes out of my total of seven. Then I cramped up and got caught behind by the mighty Kumara Sangakkara, but the Pakistan tail didn't hold up to the Lankan bowlers.

Against Bangladesh, something special happened. With my 53-ball century, we set up Pakistan's highest ODI total – 385/7 – beating another record I had been involved in establishing in Nairobi years ago – 371/4 against Sri Lanka in 1996 when I hit that 37-ball century. On the same day in 2010, I broke Sanath Jayasuriya's great record for ODI sixes.

But the politics in the dressing room never completely vanished. The captaincy crisis the team was going through since the late 2000s never really went away. Even winning the World T20 didn't bring us closer as a unit. The ups and downs of the dressing room were evident through our erratic, even inexplicable performances on the field. The batting collapses against Sri Lanka and India in the Asia Cup, all from seemingly comfortable positions, were a case in point.

There is a joke in Pakistan about the politics here.

It starts off with a guided tour of hell for a newly admitted sinner, who is being shown around his new digs by the devil. The sinner gets to one area, where there is a big cauldron of boiling oil, and in it is a man, whose head emerges every couple of minutes from the oil, screaming for help, only to be pushed back in by the devil. The sinner asks the devil what exactly is happening. The devil explains: this is a cauldron reserved for bankers; they took money from the poor and gave it to the rich, so they deserve to be in there.

Next, the sinner sees another cauldron, with the same punishment: a man whose head emerges out of the boiling oil, trying to get out, being pushed back in by the devil. The devil explains: this cauldron is reserved for lawyers; they took money from the rich to deprive the poor. They deserve to be in there.

Finally, the sinner comes to another cauldron of boiling oil, but nothing is happening with it. The oil is just boiling and bubbling on its own. The sinner asks the devil why there is no activity around this particular cauldron.

The devil responds: this cauldron is reserved for Pakistanis. I don't need to watch it. Every time a Pakistani tries to get out, another Pakistani below him pulls him back in.

20
PALACE INTRIGUES

IN THE chaos and tumult in the Pakistan team, there was a group of players that had started operating politically, even criminally. The chief among them was Salman Butt, a glamorous left-arm opener who was appointed Test captain in July 2010, before he was eventually investigated and convicted as the leader of the 'spot-fixing ring' in 2010–11. Thus began one of the darkest episodes in Pakistan cricket, where a British newspaper's sting operation exposed three Pakistani Test cricketers as guilty of corruption via fixing certain balls that were bowled in matches against England, during Pakistan's 2010 tour of the country.

A brief note about Salman Butt: before the scandal broke out, I had chosen him as my multi-format vice-captain out of a list of three. Later, after the scandal shook the cricket world, I heard that one of his many plots, even as he tried to 'buy' other players, was to get me removed from the captain's post so that he could take over the T20, ODI and Test leadership roles too.

This was painful to hear. As I have said before, I had never appreciated playing under Salman because I had always seen him as a junior, someone who still had a long way to go. Sort of how you would look at a promising younger brother with potential.

But once I assumed command and started seeing him in action, I began lobbying for him to succeed me as captain. In the days I saw my up-and-down Test career coming to an end, I often told him to be ready to succeed me as captain. That was how I envisaged him – as a future leader of one of the finest cricket teams ever put together.

After all the respect and attention I'd given him after his debut in the early 2000s and his eventual rise to Test captaincy, I didn't know that he would take advantage of the team and his position and get the talented Mohammand Asif and the young Mohammad Amir involved in criminal activities, but he did. God is the greatest judge, and only He knows what is right and what isn't, and He executes His justice against those who dishonour Him and others. What happened to Salman and the other players he led into the corruption racket is terribly sad. But it is Salman who deserves the punishment more than the others.

As I've mentioned, my approach to captaincy when faced with the larger political mess within the team was to build a sense of trust among the players. I thought that the more we met each other and talked, the better it would be for the game and the team.

It was in this spirit that I got hold of the original evidence in the corruption racket: phone messages that would eventually come into play against the players involved in the spot-fixing controversy. But when I took that evidence to the team management, what happened next doesn't inspire much confidence in those tasked with managing and running the affairs of Pakistan's national cricket team.

Here's my account: I was in Sri Lanka for the Asia Cup in June 2010 when the text messages of Mazhar Majeed – Salman Butt's 'agent and manager', who was also prosecuted – reached me, in transcript form. It is pure coincidence how I got hold of them. And it's got something to do with a kid, a beach and a repairman.

See, before the Asia Cup, Majeed and his family had joined the Pakistan cricket team during the World T20 in April in West Indies. At one of the Caribbean beaches, Majeed's young son dropped his father's mobile phone in the water and it stopped working. When Majeed went back to England, he took his phone for repair to a mobile fix-it shop. The phone stayed at the shop for days. In a random coincidence, the shop owner turned out to be a friend of a friend of mine (this may sound like too much of a coincidence but the Pakistani community in England is quite closely connected). While fixing the phone, the shop-owner, who was asked to retrieve the messages, came across Majeed's messages to the players of the Pakistan team. Though he shouldn't have seen what he did, it was that leak from him to my friend and a few others (whom I won't name) that looped me in on the scam. Soon, word got around that something strange was happening with the cricket team. It was that leak which probably tipped off the reporting team from *News of the World* as well. It was sheer coincidence: a Pakistani repairman in London who couldn't keep his eyes and mouth shut about a broken cellphone from West Indies. But I'm not surprised: when God has to execute justice, it happens in the most unexpected ways.

When I received those messages back in Sri Lanka in June, I showed them to Waqar Younis, then coach of the team. Unfortunately, he didn't escalate the matter and take it upstairs. Both Waqar and I thought it was something that would go away, something that wasn't as bad as it looked, just a dodgy conversation between the players and Majeed, at worst. But the messages weren't harmless banter – they were part of something larger, which the world would soon discover.

The rumour mill started churning. I then remembered that during the World T20 in the West Indies, Abdul Razzaq, one of our finest players in the shorter formats of the game and an old, solid hand in the team, had told me in confidence that Salman, Amir and Asif 'weren't up to any good'. I'd shrugged off his comment and told him he was imagining things, secretly hoping that their shady behaviour was just a sign of their youth and inexperience. So, when Mazhar Majeed's messages reached me two months later in Sri Lanka, they felt all the more damning, considering that a player like Razzaq – he refrained from locker-room politics – was of the same opinion: I too felt that something indeed wasn't right with Salman, Amir and Asif.

During that infamous England tour in the summer of 2010, before all hell broke loose with the *News of the World* sting of the spot-fixing scandal, I saw Mazhar Majeed and his cohorts make a re-entrance, lurking around and hanging out with the soon-to-be-accused players. For me, it was now time to sound the alarm. That's when I decided to take up the issue officially with the team manager, Yawar Saeed. I put in a formal request that Mazhar Majeed be distanced from the players, physically, and that no one in the team associate with him even on a personal level. I had my own reputation at stake as well – I was the captain of the T20 side – and feared that any controversy would harm the performance of my squad.

When Saeed didn't take action, I showed him the text messages – I'd printed them out on paper. After going through them, Saeed, taken aback, eventually came up with a dismal response: 'What can we do about this, son? Not much. Not much.'

Time stood still for me as Saeed went into denial. I couldn't believe what I was hearing from such a senior official. 'Not much'? How could we do this to the team, to the country, to our millions of fans across the world? I didn't want to believe what he told me.

Disappointed, I didn't respond or protest much. But I kept the printout with me. Saeed didn't even bother asking for a copy of it. The next day, at a warm-up game in Northampton, Mazhar Majeed and his sidekicks were again hovering around the dressing room. So I approached Yawar Saeed once more and suggested that these guys shouldn't be seen anywhere near the team, as they didn't have the best of reputations.

Middle Order:
We come from a brood of eleven. I'm number five, bang in the middle, wearing blue and holding my little sister, circa mid-'80s. My eldest brother, Tariq (extreme right) – a sensational pace bowler during his day, who would've made it far if he weren't injured – sporting a very '80s mullet, the gold-standard for many fast bowlers at the time.

Being Big Brother: That's me on the right with my little brother Mushtaq, circa early '80s in Karachi. Mushtaq would eventually join Imran Khan's PTI and try very hard to convince me to join politics as well but I wouldn't give in. I don't think cricket and politics should merge.

Fresh off the Boat: That's my younger sister behind me, circa early '80s when our family had just moved to Karachi from Khyber. Initially, my Urdu wasn't as good as my Pashto. I had trouble adjusting at Karachi's schools due to this language barrier. Eventually, my obsession with cricket would draw me further away from academics.

The King of Karachi: This was at Karachi's Jinnah International Airport on the day I returned from my debut series in Kenya in 1996. There were thousands of supporters, most of them new, some from my clubs and my neighbourhood – folks who had seen me grow up and play. This was the moment when I realized what my century in Nairobi meant for my nation and my people. Nothing would be the same ever again.

Top of the World: Following my record-breaking debut, I finally returned to my village in Kohat after having migrated from there several years earlier. This photograph was taken in 1996 on my favourite hill, just behind my family house overlooking our fruit orchards. They say that when a Pathan is not on top of a mountain, he is climbing it. It's in our blood to keep going.

The Mentor: Wasim Akram was my first captain, and the first to take me under his wing. We are seen here in Mohali, March 2016; he was consoling me after we lost to Australia in the ICC World T20. My term as captain would end at this stage but my bond with him would only grow stronger.

Cricket Diplomat: With the then Indian Prime Minister Manmohan Singh and then Pakistani Prime Minister Yousaf Raza Gilani just before the doomed 2011 World Cup semi-final against India in Mohali. I strongly maintain that cricket is the only hope for normalization of ties between India and Pakistan – nothing bonds the people of these two nations like cricket does.

His Lucky Day: We would drop Sachin Tendulkar half a dozen times before we would finally dismiss him but that wouldn't stop India from rolling past us in the 2011 World Cup semi-final to get the crown. A fierce competitor, I rank Tendulkar as one of the most resilient bastmen I've ever bowled to. Here, I congratulate him after the match, one of his luckiest.

Tearing up Toronto: Not all my innings had crazy strike rates. Here I'm seen hitting a six (one of six) in a knock of 109 off 94 balls at the 1998 edition of the Sahara Cup in Toronto. This India–Pak series was a wonderful competition in North America. My century would be the first one in the tournament which, unfortunately, is no longer held.

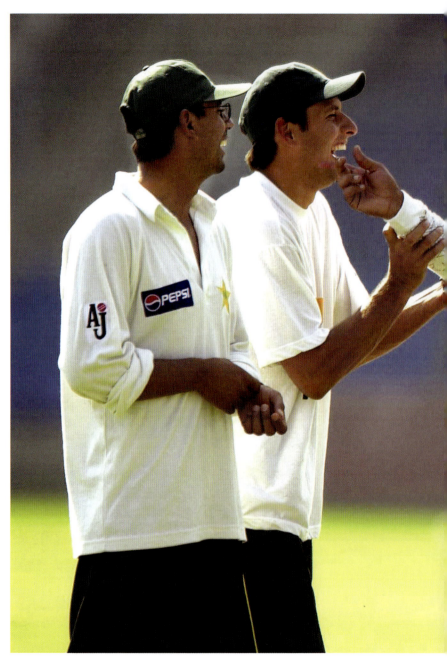

Fallen Hero: Like any Pakistani teenager, I grew up worshiping Waqar Younis. But over the years, once we began playing together, our relationship soured. I rank him as a good teammate and a below-average captain. But our falling out occurred later, when as coach, he didn't trust

me, be it on or off the field. Seen here are Saqlain Mushtaq, Waqar and I, messing around during the nets at my home ground, the National Stadium in Karachi in 2000.

Coach Confidence: By the mid-2000s, the hype over my fastest ODI century had faded away. I was confused about my real strengths: was I an opener or a quick leggie who could bat on the side? My confidence in my abilities was restored only after I met Bob Woolmer, first in South Africa and later when he became Pakistan coach. Thanks to him and Inzamam-ul-Haq,

I would finally find the right coach–captain dynamic which would help me focus on my bowling and regaining my confidence. Woolmer's words were simple but inspiring: 'Be yourself out there.'

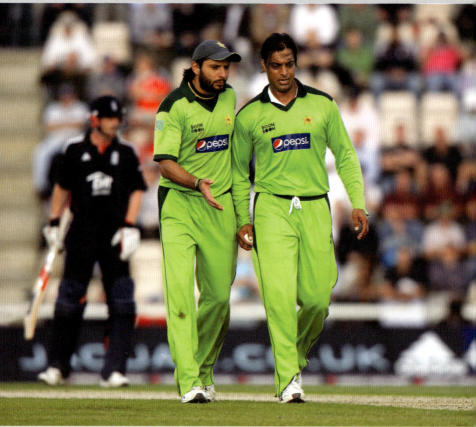

Generation Dynamite: It's tough to captain a team and tougher still to captain Shoaib Akhtar. The Rawalpindi Express was always in some sort of trouble, be it on or off the field. But since Shoaib and I are from the same generation – featuring Saqlain Mushtaq, Azhar Mahmood, Abdul Razzaq – which made Pakistan one of the better ODI sides in the world, we had a different dynamic. Together, we were always fired up. The two of us are seen here chatting during a game at the England tour of 2010, the toughest of my career because of the spot-fixing scandal.

Meant for Better Men: Even though captaining Pakistan at the Test level is a great privilege, I'm not sure I was cut out for the job. When Pakistan cricket temporarily made England its home after the attack on the Sri Lankan team in Lahore, we came together briefly but couldn't maintain our unity for long. The spot-fixing scandal would do the rest. I would lead the side for one Test at Lord's versus Australia but eventually bow out. The whites are for better men and for better times.

The Power of Prayer: Over the years, the Pakistan team would get a lot of flak for institutionalizing religion in the team's culture – something that didn't exist in the '90s. Truth be told, Islam was a potent force in keeping up team morale during some of our toughest patches. Faith kept us going, even made us bond better. The team is seen here getting ready for prayers in a makeshift mosque – the elevator area of a hotel in Colombo in 2011.

The Unworthy Apprentice: Taking young players under my wing was part of my leadership style. But nobody would dash my hopes more than Salman Butt. Seen here, at the nets in Sri Lanka for the 2010 Asia Cup, I realized something was wrong in the way Butt was conducting himself. But neither the PCB nor the coach responded to my warnings about the well-groomed, educated vice-captain. Eventually, my suspicions were confirmed when news of the spot-fixing scandal broke.

The Temptation of Khan: Who wouldn't want to work with Imran Khan? The man is a living legend. But his politics and his cricket are two different things. I admire his leadership qualities, surely. But politics is a different ballgame. Seen here, a moment from 2014, when I would help his then provincial government hunt for raw cricketing talent in my backyard, the unrestful northwest. But I would resist his call to join his controversial political protest the same year against an elected government. I would bear tremendous pressure – from my brother as well – to join Khan's PTI. But no politics for me – at least for now. Not till I have some cricket left in me.

Hail to the Victors: One of my better moments – and innings – was piloting Pakistan to the 2009 T20 World Cup win in England. In a format where my career would find a new lease, this was a crucial time for Pakistan cricket: the Lankans had just been attacked in Lahore and cricket would not return anytime soon to my country. We had no choice but to come together and we did, at the greatest of venues – Lord's. Staring at an uncertain future for cricket in our own country, we would peak in the semi-final against South Africa. The final against the Lankans would be easy. With 54 runs off 40 balls, featuring two sixes and two fours, including consecutive boundaries off Muttiah Muralitharan, I would be Man of the Match. The maturity in my innings would propel me to take charge of the team the following year.

The War Within: Despite being a whistle blower in the spot-fixing scandal and cleaning up the mess in the media that the PCB and Salman Butt had created, I would continue to perform in the field. But then the coach, Waqar Younis, would convince the PCB that I wasn't the right man for captaining Pakistan. In turn, I'd challenge the authorities and the legal battles would begin. My lawyers, one of them pictured here, held them off. But it was all quite ugly.

Pathan versus Hindustan: Celebrating Sachin's scalp with Inzi – this was the moment when it all started. I got all three of India's finest – Tendulkar, Laxman, Ganguly, one after the other – to help Pakistan clinch the third Test of that historic series in 2005. My batting was average – 0 in the first innings, and a 58 off 34 in the second – but my figures on the last day – 17–7–13–3 at an economy of 0.76 – would make Bangalore's Chinnaswamy Stadium my favourite venue in India. Victory is always sweeter against India, in India.

The Hustler: I was supposed to be a fast bowler but turned out to be a chucker. My spin bowling – more torque and muscle, less movement and flight – would develop as a default option because in my early years I would hurt a player in the nets with my faulty but lethal pace and be instructed by my coach to switch and take up spin. Still, over the years, my bowling speed and follow-through would be nothing short of a fast bowler's.

By now, the exchanges between Majeed and the players via text messages had leaked out to others. Those in the Pakistani and the larger cricketing community knew that something was up. This is probably the same period when the *News of the World* executed their sting operation.

I had done my own due diligence on Mazhar Majeed and his posse by then. Through my friends and connections in England, I'd come to know that these guys were trouble. Thus, I wasn't just making these suggestions to the management of the Pakistan team based on second-hand SMS messages, or being a paranoid conspiracy theorist. I had it on good authority that these guys, who were officially engaged in conversations with Pakistani cricketers, were indeed not up to any good. So yes, I was building a case against Salman, Amir and Asif – one that could be dealt with internally.

However, the Pakistan team management continued to be in denial and said that nothing could be done about it. Frankly, I don't think the management gave a damn. It still was nobody's problem; that's why nobody wanted to tackle it or go to bat for it. Typical obfuscation and delay tactics; the Pakistani management's head was in the sand. Maybe the management was scared of the consequences. Maybe they were invested in these players as their favourites and future captains. Or maybe they didn't have any respect for their country or the game. I really can't say.

So there I was, on that cursed tour, playing match after match, with a rough idea that something was seriously wrong, knowing that the management wasn't really interested in listening to me. I started going insane, really. We played two T20s against Australia and won both. That provided some relief, of course. Then we started the first Test, which we lost as we didn't – couldn't, wouldn't – perform.

You see, doubt is our greatest enemy. Doubts had started setting in a few weeks ago. I remember I was in the dressing room in Dambulla, for the Asia Cup, playing against Sri Lanka, when Salman

Butt got out in the second over. Abdul Razzaq warned me at that very moment that something was up. I brushed him aside and said that we all got paid enough as match fees. He just gave me a strange look and told me to watch out. In that game, I went on to score a century and forgot about his comment.

But when I came to England, I wasn't over it, clearly. I had signalled to the boys to stay away from Majeed and the likes. I had tried to talk to the coach and the management. Then the first Test began. Nothing changed. I could still see them lurking around the players and being part of the dressing room too.

In that first Test, at Lord's, I started doubting the whole project. What was wrong with Pakistan cricket? What was wrong with all of us?

That's when I decided to put an end to it, in my own way. In the middle of the match, around the fourth day, I told Salman Butt that he could take over.

I remember exactly when I made the decision. We were at 220 for 6. Marcus North was bowling. I swept and was taken in the deep. When the ball was in the air, I had taken my decision. I was done with all of this.

Yes, I shouldn't have quit my team. Yes, I should have played the second Test and not gone home. Yes, I was troubled, but I was in charge and should have done more. Much more.

So, I retired from Test cricket. Perhaps prematurely, but I had lost faith in the whole set-up, especially because the team management wasn't proactively investigating what was happening and instead letting the entire thing slide. I was angry and frustrated with everyone, including myself. That's why I didn't wrap up the Test series against Australia and decided to head back home to be with my family instead.

Yes. For the record, I gave up. I quit.

21
TRIALS AND LIARS

RIGHT AFTER the tour in England against Australia, I was called back for the next series – this time against England. I remember I was at Karachi Airport with Abdul Razzaq when I heard about the *News of the World* sting operation unfold.

Both Razzaq and I were standing at the immigration counter, just blankly staring at each other, while all of this was beginning to unravel as breaking news on TV sets all over the airport.

'I told you so, Lala,' said Razzaq to me. He himself was in shock.

'You did. You sure did,' I responded. It was an admission and I didn't want to let him down further about how the management hadn't listened to my warnings. I didn't sleep much on that flight. I was trying to imagine how bad things would be when I reached England.

After our flight landed, I didn't even bother checking in at the hotel. Instead, I went straight to the three accused: Salman Butt, Mohammad Asif and Mohammad Amir. Butt and Asif were up, in the former's room, visibly worried. Amir was passed out on the hotel bed. I asked them how they were doing.

Salman responded: 'Lala, they are trying to trap us. They want us to be scapegoats in all of this.'

I chose not to confront him, because I didn't want to be too harsh on him, considering what he was already going through. I asked him if there was anything more he was worried about. When he flatly denied all the accusations hurled by *News of the World*, I turned around and pointed to Amir and said, 'Well, you should be like him then. He doesn't seem to have a worry in the world. Go on. Get some rest.'

By the time I left the room, I knew. I could tell from their eyes – they were lying.

From thereon, the tour became hell. As captain, it was especially bad. Nothing was working out. Though just three of the guys were named in the exposé, the issue wasn't just about them. It was about all of us, the entire Pakistan camp. It was about the country, actually.

We were admonished as a unit. We were shown the finger everywhere we went. People said nasty things to us both on and off the field. Shopkeepers swore at us. Waiters in restaurants passed comments. On top of that, when we lost two ODIs soon after the scandal erupted, even the Pakistani supporters stopped coming in to watch our matches.

Still, we tried to fight on, and won two ODIs against England despite the absence of our three main players – they were suspended as the investigation began on the sidelines of the series. We won at Lord's, our biggest game in England, despite everything falling apart around us. We could have even won the series, had it not been for a dropped catch by Mohammad Yousuf in the last match. Still, by the end of the series, we got a lot of pats on our back for bringing some respect back to the team and the game because of the way we played, in spite of the allegations against our players. The victories weren't much consolation, though. Being on that tour was like being in hell.

It's easy to say that there's enough money in international cricket today that you don't have to resort to such illegal activities. It's also easy to say that you reap what you sow, and that those guys got what they deserved. But there's always context to clichés.

Things were going well for those players. They had county contracts coming up in England. They had captaincies and sponsorships coming up in Pakistan. Thus, what they did was an insult to us, to the game and to the country.

Temptation comes easily with the way the modern game has evolved and the way commercial interests are aligned with it. To be perfectly honest, Mazhar Majeed and his brother Azhar had approached me a few times when I was on tour, yet I stayed away from them because I knew they were trouble. I just went ahead and did my own thing. I never knew till much later what they were capable of. All I knew was that they were sending out all the wrong signals. Thus, as alleged by the supporters of the accused, I don't think anybody got 'trapped' in the scheme. They were all fully cognizant volunteers.

The same goes for Danish Kaneria, the spinner from Karachi who was caught in a county cricket corruption controversy, also in England. Danish is a good kid, but after I heard about his involvement in corruption from so many sources, including then PCB chairman Ijaz Butt, I couldn't help but believe the old saying: where there's smoke, there's fire.

Also, there's a school of thought that the uber-talented Mohammad Amir should never have been allowed back in the game. There are people who think that he ruined a great game – the greatest game of all, really – and let his country down. There are people who think that if you can vote at eighteen and can get married at eighteen, then you can be banned for life for being a cheat in the game of cricket at eighteen too.

But Amir never lied. He never lied to me when I caught on to what Butt was cooking. He never lied to the court when it came to the probe. He never lied to the media. In fact, he was ready to face questions.

Salman Butt, however, was the opposite. He lied through his teeth. Also – and this is why he really hurt me – he was the *captain*. He was supposed to *lead*. As skipper, he was supposed to take the fall. He could have apologized. He never did. Not just to me, but to the fans of Pakistan cricket. That's not what a true leader does. A real leader knows when to bow out.

As for Amir, yes, he was young. But he was old enough too. This has always been the argument from those who think he should not have been forgiven.

But remember: this is Pakistan. We've never set a great example, be it in cricket or in our justice system. We've always compromised. We've always cut deals. We've always left backdoors open. That's why Amir cannot not be forgiven. That's why he was given a chance to prove himself and make a comeback. And he has done so. Fabulously.

I tried to take care of Amir during the ban. I wanted to protect him. See, he never lied. He begged for forgiveness. He needed the protection. Salman, on the other hand, not only lied for years but also abused and blamed the team. He eventually relented. As captain, he should have accepted the blame. Moreover, he was educated. There was this whole myth built around him that Salman Butt is well-read, he's from a private school, he's better than us simpler, middle-class guys. We thought he was the real deal.

Unfortunately, ethics aren't learnt at school. We learn them at home. His ethics speak for himself. I'm not going after Salman Butt. I'm only pushing a larger concept – of what it means to be a Pakistan Test captain, the pinnacle of any Pakistani's cricketing career. And I'm issuing a warning again. What happened in England will happen again and again because we haven't taken hard, serious measures.

Thus, my one-line prediction about Salman's future prospects: there is no place for him in the team. Not in any team playing for the Islamic Republic of Pakistan.

As for Asif, he had other issues, too, besides those that *News of the World* exposed. Sure, he's got some mad skills with the new ball. I've never seen a better, more lethal new-ball fast bowler than him. That's my professional opinion. But you can go look up his off-the-field antics – from getting busted with drugs in Dubai to other errors, forced and unforced.

My take on the episode is simple. There was a leadership gap. Pakistan cricket has been in need of a captain since 1991. After Imran's – and maybe Wasim's – tenure, nobody has really, truly stepped up to take over. Imran's example is still cited almost thirty years after his retirement.

Why? Why can't we have a proper leader?

Why can't we have someone who will quell the politics? Someone who will stand his ground?

My only answer: the Pakistan Cricket Board.

You see, Imran Khan never had a proper team till he was allowed to make one by the board at the time. As captain, he was empowered by a board willing to put their trust in him. After all, it's the captain who has the most at stake when he leads his men on the field. Why not trust him? Why curb him? Why take his powers away?

They say that before he went to claim the crown in Australia in 1992, Imran was captaining *paratha*-chomping, mediocre street artists. But it was he who made them into a World Cup-winning unit because he had the authority to do so.

Meanwhile, I had spot-fixers and liars, thieves and robbers. Unfortunately, I had limited authority, an overbearing board and a second-guessing coach. By the time I put a good unit together, corruption hit my team. The squad went to the dogs soon after.

There is this narrative – that Pakistani players come from humble backgrounds and can't handle all the money and fame which comes their way when they hit international stardom. And it is believed that because they can't handle any of it, they either implode or go down the route of corruption and scandal. There's a counter to that narrative and it lies with the board, too.

The PCB shouldn't just be responsible for organizing tournaments and figuring out team selection. It should also be in charge of grooming players and preparing them for the real world.

In Pakistan, a lot of players indeed debut early, in their teens, and never even finish high school or attend college before turning into full-time cricketers. (Not that we have many good high schools or colleges left, to begin with.) While that itself is unfortunate, what is also responsible is the way our cricketing ecosystem has developed over the years – there's the absence of university cricket, and first-class cricket is on the decline. Thus, it's the cricket board's job to take a young talent and groom and guide him towards a bigger, more mature career in the game. If that includes making one enrol for classes in English, or public relations, or even learn how to dress up and eat with a knife and fork, so be it. Some kid from central Punjab who's breaking records at seventeen, and is a natural, must be allowed to play. At the same time, he should also be prepared and made ready for the real world, in actual cricket academies, not just left out in the wild.

Although senior players in the team have a lot to do with grooming youngsters, ultimately it's the board's job to make a proper gentleman out of a random rising star. This concept is huge in American sports. There's financial management: what you could do with all this money you're now making. There is ethical management: what to say or not to say and how to behave now that you're a public figure. In the US, sportspersons are considered assets. In Pakistan, they are left to fend for themselves and eventually written off as liabilities. What a shame.

The 2010 spot-fixing scandal tainted us all. It also created a trust deficit. The next time we were on the field playing a game and a player dropped a catch or let go of an easy wicket or even bowled a wide ball, I would have to hold myself back to not doubt him. But after the Butt–Asif–Amir scandal, we all fought really hard to win each other's trust and respect again.

We consolidated as a unit when we started asking tough questions from each other: why would you throw away your respect by being greedy when you already make enough money? Why would you disrespect your mates, your team and your country when that was all you had? These questions had no simple answers.

But we found them. And we fought back.

Well, at least some of us did.

22
PLAYERS, POWER AND FRATRICIDE

Not too long ago, there used to be an unwritten policy called 'Player Power' used in the Pakistani dressing room. The senior players were not just experienced cricketers and expected to lead the team in the field. Their views were also taken into account for policy decisions. What they recommended, the board largely accepted. They were on the inside, and their learnings mattered.

This wasn't always a good approach and personal biases clouded the judgement of senior players from time to time. Still, it worked well because that's the way cricket was always played and the team managed in Pakistan. In fact, Player Power exists as a formal or informal policy in other cricket boards and teams too. Veteran players have their finger on the pulse of the team and its capacity, and are always consulted before big steps are taken. They are always looped in before making major decisions.

But something, somewhere has gone wrong within the PCB. Somewhat recently, the board decided that it liked the 'Yes, sir' type of players, who would go along with whatever the board wanted. Thus, Player Power, for long the centre of gravity of the national team, ended, and the system changed. This really damaged our cricket. The seniors, who are the connect between the board and the players, have no input in the system anymore. This has harmed the efficiency of the team.

Here's a case study: In 2010–11, we had a very, very good team that was beginning to gel and had an excellent understanding of each other. But it didn't happen overnight. At least, not until issues between the coach Waqar Younis and me, the captain, had been resolved.

There was a back story to it. Soon after the spot-fixing scandal, there was a rebellion of sorts within the team against me. I was blamed for getting Butt, Asif and Amir caught. They wanted to push me to the side. I didn't relent. I hardened up. I had the full backing of the board and Ijaz Butt, the chairman. With his support, I started consolidating the team too, and even delivered wins in the series in the West Indies. But this was a sensitive, critical juncture, and I needed all the help I could get. This was when I really needed Waqar to back me up.

Unfortunately, he hadn't let go of the past. Waqar and I had a history, dating all the way back to his tiff with Wasim over the captaincy crown. He was a mediocre captain but a terrible coach, always micromanaging and getting in the way, trying to tell the captain – me – what to do, and even dealing bilaterally with the players, poisoning their ears. We have different personalities and different leadership styles too. It was a natural clash and it was bound to happen.

More importantly, I was let down. Teaming up with the manager, Intikhab Alam, Waqar started lobbying against me. He targeted the board and chairman. Ijaz Butt – who earlier in his tenure was very supportive of me – also fell victim to Waqar's propaganda. I was sacked while I was playing county, *after* having won the West Indies series. Nobody called or consulted me.

I couldn't believe it. My 'personality' – which was to put my foot down when schedules and training got too gruelling for the guys – was critiqued. I was deemed 'psychologically unfit' for the job. What hurt even more was that none of the guys I had stood up for previously had my back. Nobody came out to support me. When I decided to challenge the decision in court, I was all alone. Meanwhile, I was getting angry. Very angry. And it was beginning to show in my public and media interactions.

The plot was driven by Waqar Younis. Apparently, *he* was the most threatened by my approach towards the game. As I gained more respect in the squad, Waqar as coach kept losing ground. But instead of fixing his own approach, he criticized mine and started encouraging the same old bickering, partisan culture that had split up the dressing room earlier. What he didn't realize was that being vulgar, even cheap, with the guys wouldn't earn him respect. Respect earns respect, not shooting the breeze and cracking dirty jokes.

I think it's fair to say that when our rather infamous disagreements started, Waqar – or Wiqi bhai as we all call him – and I were both at fault. We learnt a lot about each other during that tense phase, when all sorts of reports, some true and some exaggerated, came out about how we personally attacked each other with harsh words and tried to get each other fired. At the same time, we also got to know that some people exploited our tension and enjoyed our altercation. It's painful to realize that sometimes the people you stand up for end up stabbing you in the back. But I won't take any names. Not here.

Frankly, I'm an emotional man. As captain, my mantra has always been: if my players are happy, I am happy. I believe that the guys who are treated in a fair manner and are happy off the field will do well when they're on the field. If I don't step up for them out there, they will let themselves and even the country down when we're playing in the middle. It was our disagreement on those tenets that was broadly the root of my problem with Waqar.

My conflict with him started somewhat like this. Without a doubt, Wiqi bhai is a legend of the game, with a reputation that is well deserved. As a paceman, he was a demigod. As a captain, somewhat more mortal. But when he was appointed coach, he fell: the guys who listened to me somehow didn't seem to listen to him, and vice versa. That was largely the premise of our conflict. Frankly, it could have been easily resolved through honest and open dialogue, and a united captain–coach front, had it not been for the various third parties that wanted us to clash.

As a captain, all I expected of Wiqi bhai was to help me and back me up as coach. What I didn't want was for him to take me on and confront me. In my view, the coach–captain dynamic should be about coach plus captain, not coach versus captain. That's just a personal opinion and I may be wrong about it altogether. United, we would have stood strong. It would have been good for the team's performance, morale and discipline.

Instead, the opposite happened. Egos clashed. And the people around him, naysayers, like the assistant coach and the bowling coach, started priming him for confrontation. It was unfortunate that we had a falling-out because Waqar Younis is a very, very good man and one of the finest cricketers the game has ever produced.

Wiqi bhai and I are okay now, thank God, but we didn't get here easily. To clear things, he and I had a very important meeting. It was after my comeback series in 2011, when I scored a 75 and took five wickets at Sharjah against Sri Lanka in the fourth ODI of that series. Even though I was injured earlier in the match, I came back that day to become unstoppable with both ball and bat, becoming the first man to score a 50 and get five wickets in a match twice. Mohsin Hassan Khan was coach, and it was he who helped me rebuild my comeback confidence.

In this particular match, after which Wiqi bhai and I made up, I would even become Man of the Match and eventually Man of the Series. Keep in mind that this was still the bitter Ijaz Butt era, and because he and I didn't get along, and because of my controversial stand against the board, there was a lot of scrutiny on me. After the match was over, Waqar, who was commentating for the match, came down to the ground for the presentation. Here, I thought it was the perfect time that God had granted me to apologize and explain myself. So I approached him, we sat down and I asked, 'Wiqi bhai, I have a simple question: do you want to live in the past, or in the future?'

He responded as I had hoped he would respond, 'The future, of course.'

I was upfront about my apology and explained my point of view to him. He heard me out patiently, offered his own apology, put out his hand and we both decided to move forward collectively.

Later, in 2014, I was glad when I found out that he was going to return as Pakistan coach. Before his return, Moin Khan, appointed team manager in 2013, asked me how I would deal with the whole thing, about working with Waqar after all that had happened between us. I said, 'I'm here for Pakistan, and so is Wiqi bhai. There's nothing in my heart against him and I don't think there's anything he holds against me. We will be fine.'

Today, Wiqi bhai and I are indeed fine. And I believe that an honest conversation can truly change anything.

Well, almost everything.

Shoaib Akhtar, at his time the fastest and fiercest bowler in the world, and I, are from the same generation of Pakistan players. We had great times together and I, both as a player and as a captain, backed him whenever he was in trouble – which was quite often. So much so that towards the last years of his controversial career, people like Ijaz Butt and Yawar Saeed didn't even like hearing Shoaib's name spoken out loud – that's how much trouble he was in with the management, mostly due to reports on his personal life, behavioural issues and even temper problems. It seemed as if he was always in the middle of a reputation crisis.

Still, I believed that as a bowler, as a colleague and as a player, Shoaib had to be given a chance, because he was that good and showed immense promise. I tried to support him whenever I could, and went out on a limb for him, irrespective of the consequences for me – like going to war with the board and Ijaz Butt himself. I have no regrets, despite an untoward incident or two that occurred between us in the past.

I remember a flare-up involving the then-not-disgraced brilliant paceman Mohammad Asif. We were at Centurion in South Africa, joking around in the dressing room, when things just escalated. Shoaib and I were sitting on the lounge chairs, and Asif was in the washroom, not too far away. Basically, Shoaib and I were having a verbal go at it, like lads usually do, and Asif – who was listening to our witty exchange – was having a laugh at Shoaib's expense.

Now bear in mind that Asif and Shoaib were really close and hunted in pairs, both on and off the field. Maybe that's why Shoaib was more sensitive, as Asif had found one of my jokes funny, not his. Thus, Shoaib lost it, picked up a bat and broke down the bathroom door, and just gave it to Asif. It was an outbreak over nothing except testosterone and boys being boys. But that episode complicated things for both of us over time. He was banned and heavily fined. Still, as captain, I brought him back, tried to put the incident behind us and moved on.

Across the world, across teams, the dressing room has all sorts of players. There are those who suck up to captains and others in power. To get access, to gain favour, to be in the 'inner circle of the skipper', perhaps even to overcome their own shortcomings and failures, these players play a lot of politics, turn the captain against other players, or even make him imagine things. That's the crux of what went wrong with many captains and players in the Pakistan dressing room in the years building up to the spot-fixing scandal.

Although it has been rumoured, I was not a part of this scheming and politics. I'm from an era where I played with big names, legends who had big hearts, and I always sought advice from the seniors while bonding with the juniors. I stood alone and still do. Yes, I had conflicts, but they were openly initiated and openly resolved. I didn't fight cold wars. But the passive-aggressive tension that was building up in the Pakistan team during those years was beyond my control.

Think of it this way. If I say something to you about someone else and I'm your only window of insight about that person, your only source about what they're up to – because for whatever reason you're not directly in touch with them yourself – then you will start forming your opinions about them just through me. If I understand this dynamic, I can use it against that person at will and abuse the access I have to your office. That's what was happening all around me, to all the players.

It was like brother killing brother. It was fratricide.

23

BATTING INDIA IS BATTLING INDIA

MOHALI. 30 March 2011.
The sun is down. The Indians have just won their fifth World Cup match against us. This one was a semi-final and has only added more sheen to their already-perfect record.

This match stands out. I'm captain of the Pakistan side. The X-Man celebration stance – some call it the Star Man – is now a standard on T-shirts across Pakistan. There's even a music video somebody's made for the World Cup, remixing it as 'Shahid Afridi'. That is about as good as it gets for me, though. I can see my career fading towards its sunset. And my dream – to win the World Cup in India – is already over.

Back to the field. Match over. The presenter at the awards ceremony asks me a question. I'm trying to smile.

'First of all, I'd like to congratulate the Indian cricket team and the Indian nation for this great victory, and wish them all the best for the final,' I manage to say. The crowd roars. 'Wahab really bowled well today but we missed some opportunities. They played better than us. We didn't make partnerships, we played some irresponsible shots and a partnership was crucial. I want to say sorry to my nation. We tried our level best and we enjoyed ourselves at this tournament.'

The crowd roars again. I walk off. And with me, our longest run for the World Cup trophy since 1999 comes to a sudden end.

That day, in Mohali, our nerves got the better of us. Sure, we were missing Asif and Amir – new-ball spearheads any team would be helpless without – due to the spot-fixing scandal, but we bounced back with a hell of an attack. Wahab Riaz, the left-arm swing specialist; Umar Gul, right-arm fast-medium; Saeed Ajmal, the *doosra* master; Abdul Razzaq, right-arm medium and as accurate as a military sniper; me … We were all firing, even that day.

Let's be honest. We lost that game more than India won it. India's cricket god, Sachin Tendulkar, was the luckiest man in the world that day. We dropped him on 27, 45, 70 and 81. He would finally be dismissed on 85.

It's almost as if his dismissal was destined to be in my hands. Or maybe not. First, he lobbed me to Misbah at mid-wicket. Dropped. Then, he plunked me to Younis at cover. Dropped. Then, Kamran Akmal pulled a Kamran Akmal, not getting anywhere near a thick edge I forced. It wasn't over: Sachin then pulled Hafeez half-heartedly to Umar Gul. Dropped.

I finally got him off Ajmal in the covers. But something was wrong that day. Or maybe everything was right in the larger scheme of things and we were part of the grand plan that would give Indian cricket its greatest moment in twenty-eight years.

For the Pakistan team, the ultimate match is always against India. Always. Regardless of where Indian cricket goes – and it's going places, no doubt – and where Pakistan cricket goes, regardless of the politics and commercial deals and whatnot, India versus Pakistan is the greatest cricket match on earth.

It's been speculated that the mental preparation that goes into a match against India is on a whole different level, that some special planning goes into each game, that the way one prepares for the match is different. All that is speculation.

The only thing which drives you in a game against India is being a Pakistani. Everything else becomes secondary – the skills, the plans. It's all about the country. I've seen it in the best players. I've seen it in myself. On game-day with India, it's all about Pakistan or bust.

2011 was our World Cup to take. We knew that if we made it past the Indians, the Lankans couldn't defeat us. I wasn't fully in charge of the team, though, and was taking on the captaincy on a tournament-by-tournament basis. My acceptability as captain was still a matter of debate – less inside, more outside the team.

There were some hiccups. I took a decision to call in Javed Miandad as batting consultant for the side. The move was aimed at providing the younger guys in the team some inspiration. It was for a motivational purpose. It wasn't meant for him to be made head coach. (Waqar Younis was.) Or a bowling coach. Or a fielding coach. Or a physio. Or a shrink, for that matter.

But he wanted to be all of that and more. Classic Javed, where the shadow is bigger than the man. He was clearly unfit for the job and our batting didn't fire when it counted the most. No doubt about it, having Javed in the squad was a disruption rather than an aid. It was my decision and a bad one.

Personally, touring India has always been my favourite thing to do on the international cricket circuit. Keep in mind that because of the shutdown of international cricket in Pakistan, we tour a lot – more than any other side – but the India tour is *the* tour. The value that cricket holds in India can't be found anywhere in the world. And the same can be said for the value of a cricketer, even a Pakistani cricketer.

An India tour is all about their people and their culture. The amount of passion, the type of fans and the level of fandom I've seen in India, I have never witnessed anything like it anywhere in the world. Cricket stars enjoy immense respect. They are considered *bhagwans*, gods. I'm not exaggerating.

As a kid, watching India versus Pakistan matches was a different thrill and invoked a unique sort of excitement. Playing against India took that very thrill, that innate anticipation that every Pakistani has, and made it into an adventure, a battle. Like good soldiers tend to do in combat, we took the lead from our seniors, from guys like Wasim Akram who, like good generals, led from the front and were themselves that much more motivated whenever we played India.

In the field, our orders for India games were simple: go and destroy them, almost like a suicide bomber does (I know that doesn't sound politically correct – at all – and *nobody ever gave that direct order*, so spare me and forgive me, but you know what I mean by that analogy!). Let nothing remain unresolved, untried or undecided.

Given the difficult political context of the times we live in, this sort of approach may sound controversial. But what I'm trying to say is that we had a give-it-all and take-no-prisoners approach to playing India. There was no ambiguity about the importance of the match, especially when we were playing them in India. Aware of the mission, be it a big match or a regular one against them, we didn't look back, nor did we care. So, sledging worked. So did aggressive body language. So did the passion of our youth. We used to take on everyone, pick a fight – a *panga* – with anyone who got in the way. The idea was not to be scared of anyone, be it a big star or an up-and-coming rookie. The mission was to take them all down not just with the cricket, but even with our body language and competitive aggression in tactics and talking. Honestly, that's how we used to take care of them, and till Indian cricketing standards really started to rise, as they have recently, our approach worked.

I've tried to study and understand the Indian team more than any other outfit out there. In the very early days of my career, Sachin Tendulkar was the only man in that unit who looked like a proper batsman. Then emerged Dravid, then Ganguly, and then came a flood of these new guys. However, all of them were groomed and polished over time, with experience.

But Sachin – he was always polished. I think he was born polished. He had his own style, grandeur and class. Eventually, Virender Sehwag and the likes joined him up there in terms of averages, but in those early days, we really used to take them all to town with our trademark positive aggression.

Before the balance of wins versus losses against India started to recently tip in India's favour due to Pakistan cricket's internal political and financial problems, till the time we retained a dominant position over them through the 1990s and well into the 2000s, our strategy was just in our heads – it was as if we knew that we would win. There was no other way to deal with India except mentally conditioning yourself for victory.

The attitude came easily and, no, we didn't have to be 'coached' into beating India. Since we were kids, the whole India versus Pakistan thing had possessed us, all of us. Even if the seniors didn't prep us with tactics for winning, we knew exactly how to defeat India on the field. The instinct to battle India was something we had internalized on our own.

Compared to other teams, I felt different when I played India. I still do. After all, it's not just a match. It's *the* match. Of course, the expectations from our team's fans, our families, our friends, are also different, much higher when playing India. It's not an exaggeration by any means when people say that India versus Pakistan is the sort of match that even those who don't know cricket are compelled to watch. Against India, it's not just a game. It's history in the making. It's the history of our people and our countries, written not in books but on the scoreboard, always to be remembered.

I can't say if I was particularly fond of 'targeting' any one Indian opponent on the field. But, to reiterate, the aggressive 'body language formula' was applied wholeheartedly and widely when it came to facing off against India. When you took the field to play India, you didn't just play eleven Indians. You played against the over a billion-people strong country itself, the thousands in the stadium, as well as the millions watching on TV. That's why all the seniors – Wasim, Waqar, Inzamam – would put their most serious game face on. And it mostly worked.

And then, there were the rivalries. Some personal, some professional. First is the curious case of Gautam Gambhir. Oh, poor Gautam. He and his attitude problem. He, who has no personality. He, who is barely a character in the great scheme of cricket. He, who has no great records, just a lot of attitude. He, who behaves like he's a cross between Don Bradman and James Bond or something. In Karachi, we call guys like him *saryal*, burnt up.

It's simple: I like happy, positive people. Doesn't matter if they are aggressive or competitive on the field. But you have to be positive. Gambhir wasn't. I remember that run-in with him in Kanpur during the 2007 ODI series when he completed his single while running straight into me. The umpires had to finish it off or I would have. Clearly, we had a frank bilateral discussion about each other's female relatives. Whatever. Gambhir doesn't matter. There are bigger fish to fry when playing India.

It should be noted though, that my bad equation with Gambhir was a one-off. No doubt, my relationship with most Indian players has been great.

So, trust me when I say this about international cricket: body language is one of the most critical components of the modern game. At the international level, everyone's skill sets converge. Everybody has a great strike rate or a great batting average or a great pair of hands. But your eyes are the windows to your confidence. If the opponent looks into them and spots a weakness, you're done.

When you're young and playing a team like India, you move and hustle around a lot in the field. If you're fielding, you go and pat the bowler as he makes his way back for his run-up. You clap hard and chant loudly: for the cameras, for the crowd, for your team, but also for yourself and the guy with the bat. If you're bowling, you extend your follow-through just a little more than usual, go up to the batsman and give him a nice little stare to make him want to go to the washroom or back to his mother.

Your tactic is your tone. Your weapon is your voice. And your eyes are your arsenal.

The idea is to have body language of the sort where the batsman actually says, 'What are you doing, mate? Let me bat in peace, will you?' *That's* when we sense fear creeping up in him. Even if he talks or sledges back at us, there is no stopping, no mercy and no end to the sledging from our end. And if you can't sledge, say, because of an overzealous umpire or something, then you stare him down like you want to eat him, then and there, like he is a piece of meat, and the pitch is a plate. That's *the game*. That's what I did against opponents, especially India, and still believe that if applied well, it can break down any opposition.

However, after many a match against India, there were some players from their side who complained about what on earth we were up to on the field. In response, we told them that it was honestly nothing personal – that's just how we played.

Off the field, however, personal connections were allowed. We used to hang out in each other's rooms – Harbhajan Singh, Yuvraj Singh, Ajay Jadeja – I hung out a lot with them. They're all great guys and we had some great times together. But on the ground, we couldn't stand the sight of each other.

It's not complicated. The rivalry is forever. They are Indians. We are Pakistanis. The end.

24

SLEDGING, TAMPERING AND THE UNFORGETTABLES

I'VE GOT into trouble many times, over many things, but I don't regret paying any fines or penalties for sledging. Aggression is the beauty of cricket. Trash-talking and sledging isn't very gentlemanly. But I can't imagine a more boring game if one doesn't indulge in teasing the opponents a little. Viewers like it too. But sledging should be limited to just the field. Sledging off the field? No way. Never. It's unhealthy.

I'm not an ambassador of trash-talking, but I used to like sledging more when I was younger. Now that I've sobered down, I treat the concept differently. However, there's a new lot in the Pakistan team who are really into it. But as an older/former teammate, it's my job to see that the young guys are well tutored in the dark art of tolerable sledging that's within limits – instead of getting noted by the umpires and the referee – and it gets the desired results.

Gautam Gambhir was my favourite sledging victim at one point just because of the way he talked back. So was Shane Warne.

They both used to get fired up and talk right back at us, so it was always more fun with them. But I've had some embarrassing moments as well.

I remember, once we were in the middle of a bad series in Australia. We were playing a tough game and I was desperate for a win because it was my first stint as captain. Plus, we were in Perth – the wicket there is never helpful to visiting sides from the subcontinent – which didn't help in times of desperation. Pakistan was in a strong position to win but needed just a little bit of extra help with the ball. So, in front of the cameras, with millions watching, I did what's probably been done before but never captured on live television. I bit into the ball. Big, juicy bites, to dent it and make it work for us.

Here's the thing: everybody tampers with the ball. Everybody. I just showed the world how I do it without really trying to conceal it. It's that simple. I wanted to win. I like to win. And I'm sorry, very sorry, that I did it. I was emotional and hungry for a win and yes, that's why I ate the ball – or tried to.

I'm sorry about that whole episode. Sure, emotions are important. They're good during an intense game. But having played for twenty years or so, it's fair to say that controlling emotions is a better bet than letting yourself go.

Was I ever terrified of a particular opponent? No. Not terrified. But there is one player who bothered me with what he could do. And he could do it all with his eyes.

Steve Waugh used to read players like a book. One look at a player and he would know what he was thinking. Even when his team would underperform, he would not give up and manage to deliver a win all by himself. They called him the 'Ice Man' and rightly so. He was always cool and calm, and it's brilliant how he knew the technique of individual batsmen and unleashed his bowlers on opponents accordingly. He was fearsome in the field. He would have made a great soldier. His tactics were his strategy and his strategy was to win, all the time, even against the odds.

As for inspiration, even though I believe that man is his own best friend and his own worst enemy, of course, legends help. They say that I'm the biggest star in Pakistan since Imran Khan. Whoever they are, they are too kind. It's great that I'm compared to an ideal I used to dream about. Imran Khan's 'Pathanpana', his Pashtun-ness, his Mianwali roots, his style, his belligerence in the field – a Pashtun trait he has carried into politics – were all very inspiring during my growing-up years. From his unbelievably athletic run-up to the craze he stirred in that era of cricket to his genuine superstardom, everything about Imran made me want to be an aggressive Pakistani cricketer.

Wasim Akram, another legend of the game, treated me like a younger brother, as did Moin Khan, Saeed Anwar and Inzamam-ul-Haq. For the teenage kid that I was, even hanging out with such stars was a dream come true. Playing with them, learning the game from them was beyond a dream. These guys are unforgettable.

If Imran was my hero, Wasim was my mentor. Fighting hard on the field, living easy off it, he is a man who demanded everything on the field and nothing outside it. During matches, he would break my back. After them, he would help me shop, put my wardrobe together, party and hang out with me like he was a schoolmate – even though he was the skipper.

My biggest lesson from Wasim bhai: fight till the end in a match. Surviving out there was – is – everything. Without a fight, there is no cricket. And without cricket, there is no purpose to life. Not for him and not for me.

There were other mentors along the way too. There was Saeed Anwar, my favourite batsman till date. He told me to never leave my core strength – power hitting. Slashing out. Whenever I was in doubt about my batting, I thought of Saeed bhai's advice and bounced back.

Of course, I was lucky to have played alongside my fellow Pathan, Younis Khan. What a hard worker! Not a talented or naturally gifted cricketer, of course, but Younis showed the world that you can go far, very far, with basic cricketing skills.

I must also mention my fellow Karachiite, Moin Khan. If there's anyone who taught me how to hike up morale, on and off the field, it was him. How to deal with the younger guys, how to motivate a bowler, how to get the team into a huddle and decide what next – I learnt a lot from him. Moin is the perfect wingman. He is also a kind man. We have done a lot of voluntary aid and development work together.

As for someone who didn't play for Pakistan but would be great to have on one's side, Brian Lara is enviable. His talent, attitude, openness and friendliness are very inspiring. We have hung out a couple of times; he lives life to the fullest. His fame, his style and his personality, his left-handed elegance: he would have been a great teammate. But, no offence to Lara, I'd never be a left-hander. If I were to start again, I'd always be a right-hander – although I wouldn't mind having Lara's natural flair. Compared to his graceful strokeplay, my shot selection looks clumsy. He is a maestro to my butcher.

Speaking of grace, now that we are on the topic of my favourites, here's my list for what would be my all-time best Pakistan XI, World XI and yes, even a Pakistan–India Joint XI. (Disclaimer: This is a strictly professional opinion. No politics were conducted or grudges held during the formation of these rosters.)

So, without further ado, my all-time best Pakistan XI:

1. Saeed Anwar: Pakistan never saw an opener like him, and probably never will. The strongest opener we've ever had. Aggressive in battle, a Karachiite in mental toughness.

2. Aamer Sohail: A brave player. Classy. You need to be brave to open.

3. Inzamam-ul-Haq: Backbone. The top of any middle order.

4. Mohammad Yousuf: Top class. Great technique. You need his orthodoxy on the field.

5. Javed Miandad: Wily. Situation-savvy. Makes the middle order tick in any condition or situation.

6. Imran Khan: Best skipper and all-rounder we've had. Period.

7. Shahid Afridi: Pathan. Game changer.

8. Rashid Latif: The toughest wicketkeeper ever born between Dhaka and Peshawar.

9. Wasim Akram: The king of the new ball, the commander of the old ball. The sultan of swing.

10. Waqar Younis: The bullet which comes in from the other end if Wasim is on from one end. You can't not have the two Ws together.

11. Shoaib Akhtar: Ferocious. Furious. Complex on and off the field, but makes batsmen think of their mothers at least twice in an over.

Without a doubt, Imran Khan would be skipper of this side.

Now, for my all-time best World XI:

1. Saeed Anwar: As explained earlier.

2. Sachin Tendulkar: World class. Legend. I'd have him open. Always.

3. Virat Kohli: This was a tough one. He's the top No. 3 guy. There are other great No. 3 guys, like Ponting, but for me, it's Kohli. You want to see him bat and bat and bat. But I'm almost tempted to repeat what a fan infamously said to him at the Champions Trophy final in 2017 in London when India lost to Pakistan: 'Kohli, *nahin hota tujhse* chase!'

4. AB de Villiers: Top-class skills. Very diverse in all formats. My kind of guy.

5. Inzamam-ul-Haq: As explained earlier.

6. Jacques Kallis: Top all-rounder. Outstanding in the field.

7. Adam Gilchrist: Great keeper, great batsman, great tactician.

8. Shahid Afridi: Enough said.

9. Wasim Akram: As explained earlier.

10. Glenn McGrath: Nobody's been more accurate with a new ball. Nobody. Plus, I wouldn't want to face him on any morning of the year.

11. Shane Warne: Can turn around any match, no pun intended.

Let it be noted for the record that Wasim Akram would be skipper.

Now for perhaps the most controversial bit: my all-time best Pakistan–India XI:

1. Saeed Anwar: Again, I love aggressive openers. He looks good when he starts. It's a treat to watch him. Plus, he handles situations well.

2. Virender Sehwag: As aggressive. Will add to a positive start. Will pair up well with Saeed.

3. Virat Kohli: World class. Great game awareness as well as self-awareness.

4. Sachin Tendulkar: The king of any middle order. The king, period.

5. Inzamam-ul-Haq: Can handle the pressure of the middle order. Crucial situational awareness.

6. Imran Khan: Captain of this side. Born leader. Best all-rounder the subcontinent has produced.

7. M.S. Dhoni: Hitter, finisher, keeper, soldier.

8. Wasim Akram: Without a doubt.

9. Shoaib Akhtar: Speed star. The terror of any batting line-up.

10. Waqar Younis: Reverse swing specialist, great partner to Wasim.

11. Anil Kumble: Natural wicket-taker. Mr Line and Length.

Let it also be noted that during my time in Pakistan cricket, I've seen a lot of potential go to waste, untapped. Nadeem Iqbal, a brilliant right-handed Peshawari paceman, could never make it, despite taking 258 wickets in 80 first-class matches with an average of 25.92. He had 13 five-wicket hauls. Nadeem had a lot of talent but not a lot of luck. So did Javed Qadeer, a solid wicketkeeping batsman. He had a lot of competition, like Rashid Latif, for example, which looped him out of the big leagues. Also, Shadab Kabir, a solid left-handed batsman and my roommate in Nairobi when I debuted, was hugely talented but also had a lot of competition.

None of that matters, though.

You can try, try and try again. But your *taqdeer*, fate, has already been decided.

25

VISUALIZATION, HEALTH AND ADAPTABILITY

THERE ARE a few bowlers out there who have bothered me chronically. They have rubbed me the wrong way. They have caused discomfort and anxiety. Glenn McGrath. Courtney Walsh. Curtly Ambrose. New-ball assassins, all of them. They knew what they were doing. They had a relationship with the new ball, like it worked for them. They could make it talk, sing, scream, even hurt. Yes, as I faced them in my younger days, maybe the fear factor was compounded. But even though we are all retired, I would be a little unhappy facing them even today. They are my bogeymen.

But here's a secret. If you're battling fears, the visualization technique works. I never did enough of it, although I wish I had.

I started it on my own in school. But it was Wasim Akram who actually made me a believer in this great habit. It was somewhere in the beginning of my career and towards the end of his. I'm not exactly sure when exactly, but it was the sultan of swing who really got me going on something I had only experimented with at the school level.

Here's how it works. The night before a big match, just when you have hit the sack and are getting ready to pass out, think about your game in clear visual images.

Picture yourself in total, grisly detail. Lacing your boots up. Strapping your pads on. Putting your gloves on. Adjusting your helmet. Loosening your batting arm. Entering the stadium. Walking to the pitch. Taking your stance.

Play the ball, the first one, in your head. Stop it. Or flash hard, depending on who you are – though you should try not to ever flash at the first ball, ever, unless you're desperate. Or a Pathan.

Keep playing, ball by ball, in your head. Play the whole damn match in your head, if you can stay awake. Try everything. Strokeplay. Defensive stuff. Aggression. Running. Rotating the strike. Breathing. Timing the ball. Do what you must. Do what you will. Visualize it all till you pass out.

I did this exercise a few times prior to some big games in my career. I'm not going to say which ones. But it really helped. Unfortunately, I wasn't disciplined enough, so I didn't do it regularly. I was careless. It's carelessness that is my biggest enemy. Who knows, I could've been a better player had I done this visualization exercise more often and consistently.

Of course, that's just one trick. You know what helps the most on the field? Confidence. It's amazing. Heaps and tons and loads and droves of it. The more, the better. I admit, I may have just a bit of it. It helps one out in many – no, most – parts of the game, even life. But overconfidence – that's fatal. It can make you slip up. It can trigger your greatest defeats.

Imagine this. You're batting. You're feeling the pressure but ignoring it. You think you're believing in yourself. But what you're not doing is getting your focus straight. You're overconfident and not observant enough. You're looking at the bowler. You're thinking he's mediocre. You're thinking he's no good. You're focusing on his past, on his stats, on the last time you knocked him around and out of the park but you're not thinking of the present threat that he poses.

You're overconfident. You don't see him coming. And you're out in the blink of an eye.

Overconfidence kills. Avoid it. All the time.

Here's the thing about Pakistan. We stop well. Or we lash out well. Thus, we do well in Tests and excel in T20s. That's the irony. Unfortunately, we are suffering in ODIs. We can't pace ourselves. We can't keep our cool. We can't turn off, switch on, go into hyperdrive and go back to cooling off. We can't finish. We can't sustain ourselves. That's our ODI gap.

It's about practice, too. You find yourself in all sorts of situations in an ODI, all within a single day. I don't think Pakistan is playing enough ODIs, to begin with. And no, it's not about captaincy. It's not about Azhar Ali versus Sarfaraz Ahmed. We have to let the new skipper have a go. We can't have these younger guys on probation all the time.

See, cricket has changed. T20 is awesome. But it's blamed for quick money and instant gratification. It's blamed for commercialization. The purists hate it. But the evolution of the game is important. Everything must change. Cricket must change and will continue to change whether the old-schoolers like it or not. That's just the way things are.

In a Test match, chances are that you can tell by the third day what's going to be the outcome. In a T20 game, you usually can't predict a winner till the last ball is bowled. You just don't know, and that's what makes the format a force to reckon with. It's like the movies. You move on with technology, right? You can't just stick to the same old sets and the black-and-white silver screen, just because it is classy and reminds you of the good old days. You have to change production methods. You have to deal with the green screen. Look at what people have achieved with CGI (computer-generated imagery). Cricket is the same.

Also, it doesn't matter what form of cricket you play, you have to stay fit. I've learnt this the hard way. You see, I'm strong. I always was. But crossing forty is not something I'm taking for granted. Upper body, lower body, cardio, core – I mix it up, every day. Or else I'll get bored. I travel a lot but still keep my trainers and gym clothes on me. I do in thirty-five minutes what other guys do in one hour. When my body gets really sore, I swim. It opens me up and relaxes me.

Once upon a time, I used to eat everything. I avoid bread and rice nowadays. I also eat only with a fork! I don't play golf. I don't do ski vacations or beach resorts. I go home, to my wife and kids. That's my vacation, being at home with my girls.

26

SHORTCHANGING PAKISTAN

I'M VERY clear about the principle of self-confidence. If you don't have self-confidence, a core belief in yourself, you don't have anything. It is in this area that I think the Pakistan cricket team, thanks to the Pakistan Cricket Board, has lost the self-belief it once had. It's unfortunate, but I'm forced to make such an assessment because of the facts.

Firstly, I don't think the PCB has anyone – not one qualified man or woman – who can stand up to or debate or argue confidently with the highest levels of the ICC, the governing body of global cricket. That's because the PCB doesn't have confidence, nor does it have a plan. And because it doesn't have a plan, it doesn't have any ambitious objective or long term-goal for Pakistan cricket.

The problem of the PCB is not uncommon in Pakistan. There aren't enough professionals within the organization. Instead, there are shortsighted bureaucrats who just want to save their own seats and skins. It's not like they don't work. Of course they do, but they don't do – can't do – anything grand or fantastic because they can't think beyond tomorrow or the day after tomorrow.

If the PCB adopts a long-term approach to the game, say for the next five to 10 years, then Pakistan cricket would be on a different trajectory of growth and development, and the nature of cricket in Pakistan would be different too. Sadly, the board thinks on a tournament-to-tournament basis and on sponsor-to-sponsor terms. It's sad because, as it limits itself, it limits the game and stifles the achievements that men – like my teammates and myself – can bring home.

I hate recommending this but maybe if a couple of foreign professionals came in to manage the PCB as an aggressive, forward-looking business unit and took up the CEO (chief executive officer) or the COO (chief operating officer) role, or any position that is empowered, then Pakistan cricket would start to look and feel different. Other multinational companies in different sectors expand their horizons and operate similarly in Pakistan. Why can't the PCB do the same with its international outreach and, perhaps, Pakistan's most globally known product and brand – Pakistan cricket?

A case in point is the controversy over the 'Big Three' issue where Pakistan cricket stood isolated in challenging the hegemony of Australia, England and India during the reforms debate a few years ago. Sure, the Big Three system is the staple now but the tale of our failure to challenge that arrangement – where the Big Three call the shots of how and where the game is played, globally, and decide who plays whom – is an obvious consequence of not just the PCB's internal managerial weaknesses but also the events in the buildup to that failure: the attack on the Sri Lankan team that choked off international cricket in Pakistan, the captaincy crisis in the team, the spot-fixing controversy and even the very real threat by the ICC that Pakistan cricket could be shut down for four or five years till the PCB puts our house in order.

Dealing with the Big Three under such circumstances has been difficult. Yet, it merely leads one to the conclusion that self-confidence in advocacy and an aggressive restructuring of the domestic and international game in Pakistan is the only way out for my country to regain its once-glorious cricketing status. Pakistan has to make itself strong again. Pakistan must rise back to the top of the field, the ratings regime and the decision-making table at the ICC.

Thankfully, the security situation in the country is getting better. Successful editions of the Pakistan Super League (PSL) have allayed fears that no foreign players would come to play in Pakistan because of security concerns. The October 2017 T20I game in Lahore, albeit with a watered-down Sri Lankan unit, partially changed that perspective. But aren't our local cricketers talented enough to bring a new energy and impetus to the game? Can they not be channelled, marketed, promoted and used correctly? There was a time when first-class cricket in Pakistan was followed widely. Why can't we take the key learnings from our local success stories and merge them with the current and best practices of the modern game today?

Till we don't get back our self-confidence, till we don't get the right people to market our cricket to our nation and rediscover the talent out there, not much will come of it. The proof is in the books. Marketing rights for a regular international series go for $150,000 to $200,000 today. Seriously? And this is supposed to be one of the greatest teams to have ever played all formats of the game?

I've had sponsors come to me and express amazement about how they came to the table with budgets of $700,000 or even a million dollars for a bilateral series, but the PCB was happy to undervalue the deal and sell it for peanuts. Is that fair to the game, to the audiences, to the players or to the team? No. And no, spot-fixing or match-fixing or player corruption has nothing to do with the problem of undervaluing and underselling Pakistan cricket. That is a serious shortcoming, shows a lack of ambition and is the fault of the people who run the PCB. This has happened under the tenure of not one, but several former chairmen. Also, to clarify: I'm not advocating greed here. I'm pushing for self-worth. If we want to catch up with the Big Three, then we must get the PCB and its finances in order as soon as possible. For that, we will have to get over our internal politics. Tall order.

27
INDIA 2.0

LET'S ADMIT it and not sugarcoat it. Things have gone from bad to worse between India and Pakistan in almost every way. The current state of affairs is ugly and hurts both nations. The trolls and the fake news on social media hurt too. Even more painful is the firing on the Line of Control (LoC) and the loss of lives on both sides, but not as much as the general breakdown in general civility between both countries. And let's not even get into how the mainstream media operates on both sides of the border.

First, policy: we have always welcomed India, in all matters related to the game. The love and welcome they've received on their previous tours of Pakistan – at least the ones I played in – have been on such a scale that I don't think Indian players will ever forget it.

Unfortunately – and I'm not talking about politics, diplomacy or proxy wars here – India has not reciprocated Pakistan's overtures.

There were days when Bal Thackeray's Shiv Sena alone would threaten our team when we toured. Now, with the Narendra Modi government in power at the centre, the hateful era of Thackeray and the Shiv Sena pales in comparison with the BJP (Bharatiya Janata

Party) government's broader Hindutva policies towards Pakistan and Pakistan cricket.

I've seen it in my hotel room TV. I've seen it in the lobby. I've seen it from the team bus. I've seen it in the parking lot, the stands, the dressing room and the ground. The anti-Pakistan narrative in India has gained heights I could never imagine. It's almost as if the hatred against Pakistan – by India's political leadership, by the trolls on social media, by the anchors on television – is not organic, but organized.

Yes, I know tons of Indians who are simply awesome. They love the game of cricket for what it really is. These Indians agree with me when I say that you can't do away with Pakistan if you're an Indian, just like you can't wish away India if you're a Pakistani. But I feel that those voices are drowning out in modern India. If we can't be friends – because of our natural rivalry – then maybe we can at least be good neighbours?

Yes, Pakistan has its own problems. Sure, there are a lot of crazy people in our country. But our elected leaders don't go around saying that they will break up India into a thousand pieces. That's the difference between their leaders and ours. This new style of politics that has gripped India is disturbing, with their leaders, ministers, even Prime Minister Modi, going on about teaching Pakistan a 'lesson'. It's also disturbing to see videos of their officials propagating violence and the breakup of a sovereign state, while not condemning barbaric acts from within, like beef lynchings, love jihad, or even dealing with populist outrage over a Bollywood flick, as happened with *Bajirao Mastani* and *Padmaavat*.

For the record, as a Pakistani, I'm an isolationist – we need to first and foremost get our own house in order. But because I'm a cricketer, and you cannot avoid talking about India as a Pakistani cricketer, the vitriol and hate from India against my country has never been louder and I must critique it. Of course, there have been ups and downs – mostly downs, unfortunately – in the relationship between the two countries. But I remember, in comparison to recent times, during the days of Atal Bihari Vajpayee sahib's prime ministership, when the same BJP was in power, things were very, very different. Vajpayee sahib's India, under his leadership, was a class apart.

Clearly, today things have a taken a turn for the worse. India's politics of democracy has morphed into the politics of populism. See, there is a difference between democracy and majoritarianism – the equitable rule of the people versus the rule of the mob. The current Indian government doesn't seem to know that difference.

If I were foreign minister for a day, I would get on a plane and go to India and tell them just one thing: calm down your internal narrative. Tell your media to chill out. It exaggerates, it lies and it creates hateful content which ruins the great game of cricket, a game both our countries absolutely love. After all, cricket is the only common love we have left, it seems. It's also the best chance for actual people-to-people contact. Cricket diplomacy has worked in the past. Why ruin that one, lonely yet potent platform?

In my language, Pashto, we say: 'Don't insult my bad mother, and I won't kill your good mother.' It means that regardless of who is at fault, regardless of who sends spies and who sends militants and regardless of who tried to break up or separate a state or a wing or a province, we need to leave a backdoor open for peace.

That backdoor is cricket.

Still, reality bites. I recall that the bad press in India about Pakistan really started during the 2011 World Cup. Their sensationalism went over the top in that tournament and really bad reporting from the Indian media became the standard norm. And then, on the 2016 tour, when I made that now-famous statement about how Indian crowds give Pakistani players more love than Pakistani crowds, the way the Indian media reported my comment, all hell broke loose. Oh, boy! Not only did that statement blow up back home – it was expected to not go down well in some sectors of Pakistan – but what hurt me was that it was taken totally out of context by the Indian media who reported that I hated Pakistan and loved India more. Unbelievable!

Here I was, trying to act like a responsible ambassador of peace – something every cricketer should do when he's on tour. Instead, the Indian media tainted my statement with harsh, xenophobic jingoism, ran it out of context and got me into serious trouble at home and abroad. All I meant to do was thank the local crowds in India for their support. It's shocking what this hunt for ratings will do to such a critical industry!

I'm not going to pin all the blame about the Indo–Pak mess on just the media, though. Context is required. 2016 was a loaded trip. Things were bad politically and bilaterally between Nawaz Sharif's Pakistan and Narendra Modi's India, and there was doubt about our tour from the get-go because of the security situation on the ground. For days, we were stuck at the National Cricket Academy in Lahore, awaiting the green light from Indian security to travel across the border. There was no contact permitted with the outside world. When our tour finally began, we were already pretty roughed up with cabin fever. In fact, there were sections in Pakistan which said that we shouldn't have been going on tour in the first place.

And then came the tour, followed by my statement, which caused more fireworks. The only Indian politician who came to my rescue was Mamata Banerjee, the honourable chief minister of West Bengal, who pulled me aside after a match and thanked me for my comments. She was someone who actually got what I had implied in my statement. Otherwise, nobody made the letter-versus-spirit distinction, and it was a real mess: a friendly comment intended to create warm ties backfired and got me into trouble both in India and back home. Eventually, after my qualifying statements – and I had to make a few – everybody, the fans, the teams, came on the same page, except for the Indian media which kept on harping about my lack of patriotism and how I was a self-hating Pakistani.

Back to my foreign-minister-for-a-day fantasy. Here's my advice: fix sporting ties with India. Now. If peace is the objective, then sports is the way to get there. Cricket. Hockey. Football. Kabaddi. Chess. Men. Women. U-19. More tours. More spectators. More cross-border traffic. Start small. Build big. Everything will improve if sports ties do. The money will follow. I dare anyone to prove me wrong. But that is *only if* peace is the objective.

Pakistan is game for such a relationship. I'm saying this because I've discussed the matter with several top officials, in and out of uniform. But if the intentions of the Indian leadership are not right for Pakistan, and if permanent hostility is on the cards, then what can one do? Nothing.

Thus, it boils down to the quality of leadership. Vajpayee sahib was a different kind of leader. A polite, thoughtful and gracious man. He loved chatting with our team, asking us questions, being genuinely inquisitive and curious about Pakistan and Pakistanis, beyond making polite small talk about things not necessarily related to officialdom. Things were different then. India too was different, I guess. Manmohan Singh sahib was a quieter man but also as nice a guy as Vajpayee sahib. Modi sahib, even though I don't recall meeting him, is cut from a different cloth. The less said, the better.

I repeat: most of the people out there in India are great. Bollywood, for example, has some of the kindest and humblest people. Shah Rukh Khan. Aamir Khan. Others. They're all so down to earth, so humble, the high achievers that they are. Then there are the thinkers, leaders, journalists, artists and, of course, the sportspersons I've bumped into. Most of them always stress on the importance of improving cross-border ties. They're so curious about understanding Pakistan. They're so worried about the lack of Indo–Pak cricket. They're actually concerned about our region, our people and our future.

But if I were to connect the dots and separate the snakes from the ladders, the current state of Indian vitriol and the absence of Indo–Pak cricket can be traced to a few political leaders and, of course, the

Indian media. Yes, politicians will be politicians. They will play to the gallery. So I will discount them. That leaves the Indian media as the single-largest barrier between a healthy narrative about Pakistan and Pakistanis. This is not a sweeping statement. There are some brilliant writers, reporters and commentators in the Indian press. And no, I'm not just picking on one country's media here: Pakistani media has got its own issues brewing. Sure, a free press is good for the country. But since the television ratings game has been unleashed, South Asian media has held itself hostage.

I must admit I'm addicted to the news. But news channels nowadays are more like movie channels. There's a lot of acting. There's a lot of overacting. There's a lot of lying. You can see the script unfold, live on prime-time television. Even though the press is crucial for the country, journalists forget that they need to be a source of inspiration, not desperation. Seemingly, most anchors and reporters are not educated and that clearly shows. They are barely ethical, too, and that shows as well. I understand the concept of breaking news. But not the concept of breaking the country or the sport or hearts. They play God, these mediawalas. This insanity has to stop.

On a side note, the BCCI needs to warm things up a bit, too, media- and outreach-wise. Whenever we have toured India, we've been very open and proactive. We give the Indian media tons of access and interviews – too bad that Indian players who've toured Pakistan have never really reciprocated.

That last tour in 2016 to India really split things open. It left a bitter taste in my mouth – the whole team's, perhaps. The security concerns didn't help. The media hype only compounded the tension. A lot of the new guys on the tour were worried, and stress worked its way into their game. But the crowds loved us. India's crowds are awesome. Possibly the most awesome on the planet. Too bad they can't elect a government that is good to them.

I have a complaint to file in India. Not the Indian people, whom I love for their support, nor the Indian team, which stands as one of the finest in the world. My complaint is to the Indian government. So here goes:

If anybody from the Indian government reads this, I hope they realize that it's not just me who thinks that what has happened to this great India–Pakistan cricket rivalry is very unfortunate. I simply don't understand what the Indian government is up to when it comes to not letting these two teams engage on the cricket field. They need to let us play more cricket with each other. Either the good people in New Delhi don't understand the true cricketing value of an India versus Pakistan match, or they don't understand that sport is actually a great mechanism for building ties and breaking down barriers. I feel that the Indian government should show some flexibility, even some sensitivity, to the hopes and aspirations of the millions – no, billions – in the subcontinent, who want India and Pakistan to play more cricket.

Also, I'm not overestimating when I say that in today's day and age, an India–Pakistan clash is bigger than the Ashes. If there is a regular, annual series, I can predict that maybe, even the World Cup will be challenged in terms of importance to the sponsors and TV channels. It's essential that we play together and more often. It's also essential for the financial future of the game.

As for the state of the contemporary game, it's unfortunate for Pakistan that the balance of the India–Pak rivalry has now tipped in India's favour. Since the likes of Yuvraj Singh, Gautam Gambhir, M.S. Dhoni and Suresh Raina came into the game, the new generation of players has pushed the old guard aside. India's fresh blood, like Virat Kohli, have really brought new life into Indian cricket.

On top of that, the IPL (Indian Premier League) has become a juggernaut and must be commended. Simply put, the IPL is phenomenal. When a nineteen-year-old rookie plays alongside Shane Warne or Glenn McGrath or Chris Gayle or AB de Villiers, and then goes back and plays for his college team or local club, can you imagine what incredible things it does for him and his confidence?

Can you imagine what sharing the dressing room or the dug-out with such global cricketing heroes does to a youngster in the game? Can you imagine how he learns from the way they play, train, eat, sleep and party?

The IPL has exposed India's youngsters to the best in the world. It is because of such exposure that there is going to be no pressure on them if and when they enter the national team. That's a major achievement because, for a young player, pressure is the real enemy, not the opposition he is playing against. On top of that, of course, Indian youngsters have received so many chances and platforms to perform at the IPL that a whole new range and generation of talent and skill sets has emerged.

Add to that India's cricket academies and sports facilities, which are now almost at par with the best in the world and designed to meet the modern cricketer's needs, and you've got yourself a rival who will keep on improving consistently. If Pakistan is serious about maintaining this rivalry and dominating over India on the cricket field again, the PCB should take note.

Our comfort zone when touring in India has shifted too. Earlier, it wasn't like that. On previous tours, I remember we used to shop, loiter around and explore like it were our own country. Such adventures have stopped now.

As for the Indian players and our relationship with them, things have evolved. There is no mercy for India on the field, of course. Off the field, we were close. Great friends, some of us. But of late, politics has seeped in everywhere.

Look at Virender Sehwag. Look at the negative statements he makes on Twitter about Pakistan. Is that responsible behaviour? Consider his fans all over the world. Consider his fans here, in Pakistan. I try to stay positive. So does Virat Kohli; he's been great. But after the recent air battles between India and Pakistan post the Pulwama attacks and the Balakot bombings, and the Indian team going all gung-ho and camo with its caps, on the field ... That was a bit much. See, we are not politicians. We are ambassadors. We can't be partisan, except on the field. In this new, hyper India, Kohli, Sehwag and Co. clearly don't get that.

Things are lukewarm, at best, now. Back in the day, we would even have each other over for a meal. During Mohammad Azharuddin's captaincy, I once had the whole Indian team over for dinner. We even went out and partied together. Now, we just pop into each other's rooms, if that's possible at all. The curfews don't help. The anti-corruption lockdowns don't help. The lack of cricket doesn't help.

Rivalries are natural in sport. But with India, they're instinctual. And with the media hype, they're accentuated further.

In my heyday, the rivalry with Irfan Pathan was instinctive. There can only be one Pathan on the field. In a jungle, there's one lion. The other one is a lioness, or perhaps, a cub.

There were healthy rivalries, too. Virat. Yuvi. Bhajji. Zaheer. We evened things out by hanging out and chilling together post-match. But in the last four or five years, as relations between the two countries soured politically, things got very edgy.

A new rivalry developed over my last years: Virat Kohli versus me. His batting was peaking when my bowling career – my whole career, actually – was culminating. For the record, there's not a better player than an Indian playing spin. This is a fact. And Kohli is one of many players in the great Indian tradition whom I have struggled against. I haven't picked up more than two or three wickets on an average against them. The Bangalore Test in 2005, which we won, was an outlier. There were a couple of other matches too. But by and large, the Indian batsmen largely remained on top of my spin, throughout my career. That's just the way it is.

But we remained on top of their pacers.

Life has a funny way of working things out.

28
THE DRY TALENT PIPELINE

GET THIS straight. Cricket isn't about making money. It's about making players. It's about making winners. It's about building assets. And assets need investments. You can't just keep hoping and praying that God will keep churning out talent. Yes, He has been very kind to Pakistan cricket and we have more raw and exciting talent, pound for pound, than any other country. Everybody who knows or plays cricket admits this. But the PCB is really pushing its luck with this 'raw talent will always rise' narrative.

That's just one diagnosis for one of the several ailments the PCB suffers from. As I mentioned earlier, a quick-fix prognosis is to get an outsider to head the board. Someone who can give the fat cats the stick. Someone who can overhaul the system. We need a systemic as well as a structural shake-up. We need an oil change. We need new leadership.

There is no consistency in the board's functioning. The entire system changes when the chairman changes. Can you believe it? It's as if we are a political party or something, not a cricket administration.

Worse is the politics: in 2015–16, we had two chairmen – one semi-retired and one semi-appointed – so, essentially, we had two systems!

Look at the chairpersons of boards in other cricketing countries. They don't behave like selectors. They behave like grand old PR (public relations) men, diplomats, lobbyists even, to keep relations with other cricket boards smooth and intact. We need a solid, respectable chairman, who doesn't meddle with the inner trappings of team selection. We probably need a *gora* CEO under him, to run the system. And we need a free and independent selection committee. You don't just pick a kid for nationals after watching him score a 50 in a local game. Or because you saw a clip of his innings on social media. Yes, you can pluck bowlers while they're young. But not batsmen. Batsmen have to weather the storms of local cricket before they can sail on the big international seas. That's why Australia rotates bowlers aggressively, but not its batsmen. Batsmen are long-term investments. They have to be grown, not plucked.

India has done better than us in this regard. One, they invest their money back in the game and don't just blow it on fat-cat salaries. Let's do some number crunching as an example. We have one National Cricket Academy, in Lahore. The Indians have a cricket academy in almost every major city. We can't make even one function properly in four provinces. They have 29 states and at least half of those have international-standard facilities in at least one ground. The Indian talent pool is, therefore, better filtered by the time a player makes it to the international level.

Also, the Indians know how to get the best out of a player. You'd think that once a cricketer has retired and the media has written him off, he would be done with the game. But he's still got other uses. Whoever is cycled out is cycled back in, if he's worth it. Ganguly, Dravid, Kumble: they have been transitioned into consultants. They've become coaches, mentors, even dressing-room big brothers. There are a hundred ways to use your older, wiser stars. India has figured out quite a few solutions in this regard. Good for India.

Meanwhile, on our end, most of the fat cats sitting in the PCB offices have never played the game. They couldn't jog a mile with the boys if they had to. Naturally, they're not going to be inspiring icons. They're only going to subtract, not add value. I won't take names but we all know who these people are. We can spot them from their tailored suits and bulging waistlines.

Sorry, I'm being harsh. But this is cricket. It's my whole life. I've never done anything else but play cricket. Hell, I even dropped out of school because of it. For me, it's simple: the game has to be run by us, the cricketers. This is our game and I'm not going to watch it fade away because of bureaucrats and political appointees. Without a doubt, the system needs an overhaul.

The golden years we pine for – the era of Imran Khan, Zaheer Abbas, Sarfaraz Nawaz, Javed Miandad, Wasim Akram, Waqar Younis – won't return till we create some new legends. One reason I'm sceptical about that happening is due to the lack of great new players. And great new players are not coming on the Pakistani roster because school cricket is dead or almost dying.

Commercialization has a lot to do with it. With the collapse of public education and private schools proliferating, there is not enough attention on sports or other extra-curricular activities. Private schools concentrate on exam preparation and academics. That's it. Public schools are a lost cause but they're the ones with the grounds and the acres. However, nobody wants to go there. If we want to save cricket, we must rebuild school cricket, from the ground up, back to the level in the era when I was playing in, when even ordinary public schools were producing great cricketers.

Parents will have to change their mindset too. When my parents sent me to school, they were open-minded about what I wanted to be. Yes, I didn't hit the books very hard but I was never arm-twisted to focus on becoming a doctor or an engineer (I was roughed around by my father, but he eventually got over it). And even the non-elite, public schools gave you options. If not the best library, public schools at least had very good grounds.

Today, schools are a business. They don't even have proper fields for sports and extra-curricular activities. The privatization wave of educational institutions has a lot to do with this. Schools are like mints now. The private ones are export factories, preparing our kids to go abroad to American and British universities, while the public ones prepare them for local servitude and mediocrity. This has to change. Or else, where will kids start playing organized sport in the first place?

The Pakistani formula for cricket till the recent commercialization of school education, much like the rest of the world, was simple. There was school cricket. Then district level, followed by college level, university level and then first-class. Then the national level. It was straight and simple.

Nowadays, as the demands of international cricket have changed, we will have to pivot our preferences and facilitate a change in the way the game is organized for our kids. We will have to change the way they are schooled so that young lads learn cricket from the ground up. It shouldn't be the case that a player begins re-establishing his basics once he's part of the Pakistan team. He shouldn't be picked out of the rough. He should be a polished diamond by the time he's ready to enter the big league.

It was all so different in my early days in cricket. When I began playing with the very legends I would dream about – of course, I was nervous as hell playing with them – the seniors used to take care of you, like big brothers do. Yes, there was dressing-room politics, but it was lateral, not vertical: senior versus senior, junior versus junior, not senior versus junior. Yes, there were rivalries within the team. But we would leave it all behind when we came down on the field. Once we had laced up our boots and were set to play, the unit would stick together. And by the way, the lack of media attention, especially the narcissism-driven social media, made people more focused too.

Imagine the greatness I was exposed to. Saeed Anwar. Ramiz Raja. Saleem Malik. Ijaz Ahmed. Aamer Sohail. Moin Khan. Rashid Latif. Inzamam-ul-Haq. Wasim Akram. Waqar Younis. This was the line-up I started playing with. Shoaib Akhtar, Saqlain Mushtaq and I were the lucky ones, the last of the lot who played with the old-school greats.

But as all these stars faded away, Pakistan's fortunes started dwindling on the field. In the dressing room, it was worse: there were no role models. And at the nets, a disaster was unfolding – the talent pool was drying up.

Back in the day, it used to be easy to play for Pakistan. It was first-class cricket where you made your bones. It was there that quality mattered. People knew who the best players were, across the board, across cities and clubs. First-class cricket was even covered aggressively by the national broadcaster and press. By the time you arrived on the international stage, you were already established nationally. Your reputation preceded you. That's all gone now.

I said as much to the BBC, about talent drying up. Again, I was quoted out of context by local media in Pakistan – clearly not just an Indian trait – that there is no local talent emerging from within this current system. Why? Because the current system is flawed. Why? Because a youngster who is coming into the game doesn't have the facilities he needs at the grass-roots level.

Consider this – only when a youngster has been picked for the Pakistan team does he start training. Training to eat. Training to field. Training to train! With all due respect to the managers and experts at the PCB – and most of them don't deserve much respect – there is no time to train when you've arrived at the international level. At that stage, it's all about performance. It's about excelling and peaking, not learning. Yes, you probably have to unlearn a shot or two, but it's not a stage to pick up new skills. The international level is where you have to harness the skills you already possess. But our system is such that youngsters pick up things *after* they are inducted into the national team, not before. The PCB has made the system run backwards.

Also, nowadays the incentive for becoming a cricketer has changed for some – and not just in Pakistan. Firstly, the money. Cricket is more commercialized than ever before. It's played for the wrong reasons by many.

Secondly, stars aren't groomed properly. There's an aggressive revolving door. New talent emerges and is routed out and dusted off as quickly if it doesn't perform. It's all a business now. You play for money and you're treated like a commodity.

Building a good national team is like building a family. It's simple, really. Once your system is sorted at the grass-roots, where a U-14 or U-16 player is getting all that he needs to excel, then you've naturally taken care of talent required at the highest level – the national level. You can't hope to have a line-up of healthy, strong sons if you don't feed them as babies. So India's secret – and it's not really a secret – is that it has taken care of the bottom of the system, and therefore it can look after its young and upcoming stars.

As for Pakistan, if we are interested in consistency, we will need to replicate and even improve upon the Indian system. Currently, we are in this permanent back and forth, in and out of good runs and bad patches. A good series here, a terrible whitewash there, two bad years in Tests, one good year in ODIs, a trophy and then a scandal, and round and round we go. People call it Pakistani flair; I call it consistent inconsistency.

We must ask ourselves – do we want Pakistan cricket to be the way it is, without a stable growth trajectory, always through ups and downs, or do we want to excel consistently? If nothing else, even if we plan on playing regularly against India, if not for the sake of our rivalry but for the country and ourselves, we will have to create a new system of cricket.

Having said that, I'm not the sort of guy who only blames 'the system' or 'the machine'. It's time for some other admissions.

Our cricketers have issues. We all do. I will be the first one to admit mine. The biggest problem is related to our ambition. Once he makes it to the national squad, the typical Pakistani cricketer wants to play on forever. Only the might of the selection committee and/or political intervention can dethrone him. Given a choice, a national-level cricketer would play on till he was 50 years old if he felt like it. He wants to hold on to his place in the team at all costs.

This is pure selfishness. Our players don't want anyone else to rise and replace them. Thus, there is no co-practising, nor any mentoring or grooming or tutoring where, say, an old star like Sachin Tendulkar will help mentor a rising star like Virat Kohli. The Indians have this approach. We don't.

Everybody has a natural tendency for self-preservation. But I'm not talking about survival instincts here. I'm talking about the habit to worry more for ourselves and less for the team and the future of the game. This is a shortsighted approach based on immediacy and is used by those who can't see beyond the short run. There is no big-picture approach to the game, something for the long haul where cricket can actually grow. It's all about 'me, here and now'. It's not about others, the next generation and how the game must change. It's about today, not tomorrow.

That's not how you play the game. That's not how you live.

This mentality is our collective problem. I'm a part of it for sure. But it's also a problem of the PCB. The PCB should be proactive about figuring out the next steps for these great, talented cricketers who have given their best years to the country and are now past their prime. They all need a graceful retirement plan that protects both the game and the player.

If the PCB could call a once-great player, sit across the table from him, pay some attention and ask him his plans about the future, such a conversation would make him and the board feel a lot more secure. An open and honest dialogue would give both the cricketer and the team options and grant some much-deserved respect to the cricketer too.

This is just a suggestion and I may be wrong about how practical such an approach is. But playing in uncertainty can destroy the most confident cricketer. The PCB needs to understand this. Confidence makes kings.

29

PREDICTABLE
UNPREDICTABILITY

THERE'S A recently devised and statistically backed allegation about me that's been doing the rounds for years: Shahid Afridi does not push himself to perform often enough. It is also alleged that I am deliberately inconsistent in my batting and let my average slip until the exact moment where I'm out of options, cornered and, essentially, have an empty can left. A certain writer even called me 'a human ATM card', someone who knows exactly when he runs out of cash before refilling his account with a good knock.

In summary, the stats basically seem to suggest that only after a series of extreme lows do I give an impressive performance that gets my credit and ratings back to normal.

These aren't unfair allegations. And I'm not railing on about being the good guy and becoming self-critical here. While I admit that it is a correct assessment, I also regret not being consistent enough. Honestly, I wish I'd never given observers an opportunity to make such an assessment in the first place.

God has made everyone differently. He tests them in His own way, and they test themselves and fail Him or themselves in their own ways. But I'm lucky. I've always got the wake-up call at the right time. And whenever it has come, I've answered it and addressed the issue. So, in all fairness, I have performed.

Overconfidence is a strange thing. It leads to a certain sort of self-contentment, a sort of relaxation that gets to your head, which makes you say, 'I've been there, done that, and don't really need to do more.' Then one day, reality whacks you on the head and you wake up again.

This happens to a lot of players in sport; it happened to me too. Broadly, it's an issue of inconsistency, so obviously it's bad news for cricketers and their place in the team.

But I acknowledge that it is this inconsistency that has become a part of my style, and not necessarily in a positive way. Perhaps one way to look at it is that it is Shahid Afridi's own style and cricket would be boring if we all played and acted like each other, wouldn't it?

Of course, there are regrets. Although I lost myself to double-minded confusion – the focus between batting or bowling – which dominated my game after that early peak in performance in 1996, I had a distinct playing style. Once I lost it, I never really got it back. I have a particularly aggressive individual talent that I should have developed and polished and not played the game the way everybody else played it. And I wish I'd been coached by someone who would have used my original, natural skill set and done something with it, instead of trying to turn me into a traditional player from an era I don't know much about and never belonged to.

Still, I soldiered on and had my share of ups and downs. The larger plan to keep going was built on the motivation I got from my trusted friends and family. They knew me better than I knew myself, at times. They knew I still had some cricket left in me. Most importantly, they knew I could do more.

That's when I eventually turned things around for some famous comebacks. I like comebacks. Otherwise, I know there were at least two times in my career when I gave away my cricket gear to friends. But my wife, my brothers and, before he passed away, my father, insisted that I continue to play on. It's all I was good at, my father would say. One of us is going to be a great name, he would tell my siblings and me, when we were kids. Even after his death, I doubt if it was me he was referring to.

As for those multiple retirements which have so often been criticized, questioned and even been made the butt of jokes – a commonly heard one was that I retired as many times as I got Man of the Match awards – well, they happened because my emotions got the better of me. When I wanted to play Tests, the powers-that-be wouldn't let me. When I made it to the Test level, they pulled me out of ODIs. When I concentrated and did well in ODIs, they dropped me from the Test team. Obviously, I reacted.

In hindsight, I can say I overreacted. I didn't accept the team selection decisions rationally and on being dropped and moved around so often, announced my retirement prematurely, even rashly. I did it again and then again. Bad moves, all of them. But I should've known: I was too passionate to quit. That's why I kept coming back. Thankfully, I was also passionate enough to not play any political games with the board or in matters of being selected.

My unorthodox style of playing and the complications it caused me, personally and professionally, are life lessons. Time is a teacher. It teaches you patience. It shows you where you went wrong. The good things you keep; the bad things you discard. So, even someone who is naturally aggressive like me ends up learning how to control the aggression, harnesses it and channels it in a better way. Sometimes, it's too late. And sometimes, like it happened at the 2009 World T20, it comes at the perfect time.

Thus, my batting is like my life. A bad innings is like a bad episode with friends who are not really friends. You make a mistake, you get out, you try to learn and move on. An evolved human being, in my opinion, is one who learns with time.

To address the most common criticism levelled against me, a lack of technique, I must point out that a lot of top cricketers lack classic orthodox technique and they still do just fine. There are also plenty of batsmen with conventional technique but they don't have the variety in shots that guys like me do.

God doesn't make anybody perfect. I'm grateful for what He has given me in terms of talent. I didn't even imagine that I'd play for over 20 years for Pakistan, serve my country doing what I love – playing cricket.

God has given me more than I ever hoped for. God is the greatest.

30
TEMPERAMENT, TRUTH AND LEADERSHIP

I'VE BEEN hearing it for years. I've been blamed for it often. I'm rebuked for my shot selection because of it. I'm chastised for my locker-room behaviour because of it. When I show a seriousness of intent, I attract sniggers because of it.

It's the ghost that's always in the attic. It's the elephant in the room. It's my 'temperament problem'.

Even though my friends are kind and say that I've changed the game due to my temperament, I realize I am an emotional man. Back in the day, I was more emotional than I am now. I've made mistakes because emotions got in the way of rational thinking. It now reminds me of the old Pashto saying: 'Don't make promises when you are happy. Don't take decisions when you are angry.'

Today, I wish I'd paid heed to such wisdom. Perhaps it would have made me a better player or a better person.

Everyone makes mistakes. But when you make a mistake, the most important thing, first and foremost, is to accept it and assess what went wrong. Then, you must fix yourself pronto. Time adds value to maturity. Let it come. Such maturity comes early to some. For us Pathans, however, maybe it takes longer. I think it has come to me, finally. I sure as hell hope so.

But the truth must be told. Under all and any circumstances. The truth needs backing. The truth needs support. There's not enough truth in the world. The truth needs to be upheld. Maybe this is easier said than done because I've always taken pride – sometimes foolishly – in not being a yes-man. I must admit, even push, that the truth must be told. Always.

There are people out there who take U-turns. Some take them for a living. Politicians, for example. Usually, one can catch them performing their little magic tricks of deceit just by their facial expressions, be it in a private meeting or at a press conference. You can even tell if they are under someone else's influence. It's a different kind of expression for each lie.

God, I hate politicians.

Anyway, even when I've tried to, say, not be myself – diplomatic, oblique, indirect, even not necessarily straightforward about what's on my mind – people who know me and even people who don't can easily catch on to what I'm up to. That's my personality. That's my thing. I don't know if it's a weakness or strength. But it is what it is.

Sure, people become sober with age. I know I tried. It's natural. I can't satisfy everyone with my behaviour. But one can only try.

Pakistan is a tough place to tell the truth. My temperament is not suited to this country's culture of being scared to face the truth and general deceit. Not a lot of people will back you if you're on a mission to tell the truth. I've learnt this the hard way.

People, even important ones, have come up to me and said, 'Listen, you have a point and it may be the truth but don't bring it up on television.' At which point I have wondered, sometimes aloud: how else should I bring up the truth then? Alone? In a room? To the walls? It's been tough, this entire experience of trying, meagrely, to be honest and aboveboard. Thank God, I've been blamed for being a lot of things but never for being dishonest. I hope I can retain the ability to call a spade a spade. I just wish I stop getting into trouble for doing so.

On the field, my temperament has both helped and hurt us. In cricket, controlled aggression helps, especially when you're leading a team. If you're the captain and lack the aggression which the moment or the phase of that match demands, then you're done for. All eleven of you.

Attitude is contagious. And aggression – controlled aggression, I must reiterate – helps. Frankly, I think Pakistanis need a little bit of such calibrated aggression from their leaders. It's how we are structured as a people. Look at Imran Khan. He's the perfect example to bring up here. How's his political party faring? Not badly, eh. One reason, of course, is that he's not corrupt, at least not financially. Period. Let's hope things remain that way.

But the second element is his controlled aggression, combined with charisma. People love it when he speaks his mind. He does it so aggressively. He's a natural crowd-puller. I can't be classified in the same category as him, I'm nowhere near his status. But if, as prime minister, he aspires to improve Pakistan, all power to him. The truth needs a teller. I don't know if it's going to be him. But I hope Imran's leadership is good for Pakistan's future.

No doubt, Imran Khan has done a great deal for fighting corruption. What a movement he has led in Pakistan. But the question is: is his own house clean? If so, are his associates clean? Is his party, Pakistan Tehreek-e-Insaf (PTI), clean? That's a long list of very important questions. To really retain the moral high ground, Imran Khan will have to answer all those questions. If your own house isn't clean, then you don't look very good shouting at the other guy to clear his yard.

But my biggest gripe with Imran Khan is that he hasn't done enough for my hometown, Karachi. Nor have the rest of the cricketing powers.

31
THE LOST KINGDOM

SO FAR, the Pakistan Super League has done well. It had to. We didn't have a choice, especially with the Indian Premier League and the Bangladesh Premier League (BPL) preceding us in the subcontinent.

With the PSL, strategically at least, we have achieved our goals. New talent has emerged. An example from the first PSL is Hassan Ali. Another one is Mohammad Nawaz. These boys are a living testament to the overdue emergence of young, fresh talent. But Pakistan's biggest problem still remains our batting. Despite the PSL, not enough promising batsmen are emerging. But bowlers are. If you ask me, I think this is a geographical issue. I know it sounds a bit far-fetched but bear with me. I have a theory about this.

I call our batting problem our Karachi problem. Karachi – our biggest, toughest, roughest city by the sea, in the south – was famous for its batsmen. Meanwhile, Punjab, our great province in the east, has traditionally been famous for its bowlers. There was an easy 'division of labour' between Karachi and Punjab. Simple.

I'm not sure how this specialization started but it was well in place by the time I started playing. We Karachiwalas batted well. The Punjab boys, and boys from further up north, bowled better. It's just how things worked. It was in our blood.

But as the developmental disparity between Karachi and Punjab kept climbing, so did our cricketing standards. One issue was the nature of cricket academies. Lahore has the only functional academy in the country. Multan, in southern Punjab, is getting one too. Karachi's academy hasn't been inaugurated despite almost a decade of trying. Blame bureaucracy. Blame the rule of the Pakistan People's Party. Blame apathy. Blame the shitshow that is Karachi.

But also: blame trends. The disappearance of cement pitches – a Karachi-centric phenomenon, although it can now be found nationwide – has hurt our batting standards.

Cement pitches improve your batting. The ball comes in fast and hard; even a medium-pacer can end up hurting you with the extra bounce a cement pitch offers. The irony is that playing in Karachi gets you ready for Perth. You learn how to cut and pull, not just lug the ball around but defeat the pace and counter the bounce. Yes, the ball gets old quite soon. However, now that's all done away with, due to the introduction of turf.

With turf, especially with the new fail-safe kind they have in schools and clubs, there's barely any bounce above your knees. So the bloodline of hard-cutting, big-slashing batsmen in Karachi has thinned out. We don't make any Saeed Anwars anymore who can rip a cut shot to the last stand of the Melbourne Cricket Ground (MCG). No longer are we physically prepared to play in South Africa or Australia, with their hard and fast wickets. By upgrading to turf – which is cheaper to maintain – we have hurt our batting prospects. That's a part of my theory about our batting woes. Of course, for the larger oversights in Karachi and the loss of its great batting tradition, I blame the Pakistan Cricket Board.

This is how the infamous decline in our batting standards is connected to the loss of our prized national possession: the city of Karachi. In my theory, the cricket connection of this city by the sea, one of the world's largest megacities, is with cement. Maybe it's because Karachi is a concrete jungle.

Consider these men – Zaheer Abbas, Iqbal Qasim, Saeed Anwar, Asif Iqbal, Javed Miandad. I've followed their career through and through and have reached one conclusion. The main logistical and technical reason the Karachi boys rule the roost of Pakistani batsmen is because of the high bounce, no-nonsense cement pitches we grew up playing on.

It's also a mentality thing. Guys from Karachi are street-smart. They're mentally tough. They're probably more educated, statistically speaking, for that's the ethic in Karachi. That matters on the field, when you're cutting and pulling and slashing, be it in Perth or Brisbane. Compared to Karachi, Lahore is, well, more of a village, like the rest of the Punjab, while the north brings in the raw energy of the rural areas, which is why better bowlers have always emerged from there and from further north, like Khyber Pakhtunkhwa. It's in the water. And it's in the blood.

But let's be honest and not play the victim card. Karachiites lost Karachi. Nobody else can be held more responsible for nearly destroying Pakistan's biggest city than Karachiites themselves. We could have made it like New York or London, a real megacity. But an elder generation lost it for us.

So prevalent is crime in my town that no family in Karachi can claim it hasn't suffered an incident or some form of trauma. I'm one of those. I remember an episode from the mid-1990s when I was just starting out in cricket. I had borrowed a motorbike – a brand new Honda – from my brother for a match. I was near the crowded Ayesha Manzil, hungry, and pulled over to get something to eat from a *dhaba*. I went in, picked up a snack, came back out and saw two guys sitting on my bike as if it was their own.

I asked them to get off the bike, thinking they might have mistaken it for theirs. The guy on the pillion seat pulled out a shiny 9 mm pistol, pointed it at me and didn't say a word. The other guy, the soon-to-be driver, put out his empty palm. I knew what was expected of me. I gave them the key and backed away, slowly. I didn't want to be a hero in a bike robbery. Worse things have happened to better people on the streets of Karachi. This happened in 1995, just a year before my international debut.

The crime wave that started since hasn't stopped. Karachi has turned on to itself, like a crazed animal. Unfortunately, Pathans have been unfairly treated there. It's unfortunate – Karachi runs the country and churns Pakistan's economic engine.

But the city is also a proxy battleground. That old school-of-hard-knocks gives us Karachiwalas an edge, a special type of determination. If I were from Peshawar Cricket Club, I wouldn't be who I am. Javed Miandad wouldn't be the hustler that he was; Zaheer Abbas wouldn't be as cosmopolitan as he was; Moin Khan wouldn't be the street fighter he was; nor would Saeed Anwar be the slashing assassin with the bat.

Karachi gives you grit. It gives you fortitude. Most importantly, it gives you claws, because you need them to walk its rough streets and climb its high walls. That's why Karachi boys are smart. Despite the bad schools, shabby streets, the polluted water and the wave of crime and terror, Karachiites are survivors. Ironically, my fellow citizens are still the most professional compared to any other place in Pakistan. Other cities seem like villages compared to Karachi. We Karachiites have the best work ethic and, hands down, are the hardest-working people in the country. We're a true melting pot of the country: Biharis, Bengalis, UP-walas, Pakhtuns, Balochis, Punjabis, Siraiki-speakers, Gujaratis, Memons and the Sindhis. They all break their backs every day to make Pakistan tick. Too bad they have been offered cards of wrath by successive governments and political parties.

Since we're talking politics, might as well get off the political fence here. This might shock a few people but in my growing-up years, I was fine with the feared Mohajir Qaumi Movement (MQM). I know they are really controversial now, and were even involved in terrorism. However, the '90s changed the MQM and the MQM changed Karachi. They did a lot of good work, no doubt, in Pakistan's greatest city. They were and are the most organized party in Pakistani politics. But they have changed since then. They have hurt the city and the people that made them.

Political violence is unacceptable. It's no good. There's enough violence in Pakistan. And organized political violence is unacceptable, in my opinion, unless you're fighting for your own country, which I hope the MQM is not.

But Karachi can't get worse than it is at the moment. I'm hoping my city will bounce back. The onus, however, is on the Pakistan Tehreek-e-Insaf to fix things. The Pakistan Peoples Party (PPP) has run my adopted province, Sindh, but the ball is now in PTI's court to deliver and make change happen. If they want to make a political comeback, they will have to fix things, for sure, and not just get charity votes in the names of the slain Bhuttos. The electorate is increasingly aware and smarter than it looks.

Yes, this is all sounding political. It should. Every citizen has a political responsibility. And a right to express his or her own opinion.

32

POLITICS AIN'T FOR PATHANS

I'VE SEEN them all.

The CEOs, the chairmen, the presidents, the prime ministers, the pretenders. I've seen them all off too.

I once had a face-off with Ijaz Butt, an interestingly flawed former chairman of the PCB. I remember: the vultures were circling. I was close to being chucked out of the national cricket team again. And guess who popped up to offer help: Bilawal Bhutto Zardari.

The offer was interesting. In return for resolving the conflict with Butt, Bilawal's people said that I must accompany the young politician on rallies. Needless to say, I didn't take Bilawal's help. Let sleeping dogs lie on that story about the negotiations. But, on the political front, I think Bilawal has a long way to go. Unfortunately, the Pakistan Peoples Party perished with his mother, Benazir Bhutto sahiba. His father couldn't hack it. That's the honest truth as I see it.

When I met him in London, Bilawal was making a political pitch, asking me to join forces with him, even campaign with him. Personally, I met him only because I wanted to meet Benazir's son, hoping he would walk on the same path his late mother did. But I soon realized who was calling the shots in the PPP. Bilawal Bhutto Zardari was just a front, I realized. His hands are tied like a puppet's. He may eventually be leader of the party, but for now, his father is in charge. That still seems to be the case somewhat.

On the other side of the aisle: Mian Mohammad Nawaz Sharif, the former prime minister. Mian sahib too offered me a position in his party, the Pakistan Muslim League (Nawaz) (PML[N]). He made the proposal rather indirectly, in his particular style, by asking me to put a lion's sticker on my bat. The lion, of course, is the symbol of his wing of the Pakistan Muslim League. I laughed it off. There's no space for politics – not on the field.

Then, of course, is that famous moment when, before he became prime minister, or was even close to it, Imran Khan offered me to join his cause openly, during his months-long 2014 protest in Islamabad.

Those were trying times for the country. Pakistan stood polarized. On the one hand, Nawaz Sharif's juggernaut had taken over Punjab, with a massive majority in the 2013 elections. Opposition leader Imran Khan had managed to win only one out of the four provinces, and wasn't doing too well. He claimed Nawaz had cheated. Nobody – not the courts, not the media, not the people – bothered to do anything about his complaints. So, he put a rag-tag coalition together and decided to march upon Islamabad. The momentum and number of supporters he required to paralyse the capital, he never got. So, he started talking to the media and pulling these interesting political stunts. Every night, for three months, as he stayed parked outside Parliament on a container, he would make some controversial speech or the other or pull a stunt. And then, one monsoon night, as he stood there with millions watching, he invited me to join him. The issue was so loaded and the country so politicized that all of a sudden, I started getting calls – from news channels, from politicians, from family members – advising me to go or not to go. The fate of the country hung in the balance with Khan's anti-Nawaz sit-in.

I decided to opt out. No doubt, Imran bhai is quite the leader. But there are a lot of people in his Pakistan Tehreek-e-Insaf whom he doesn't need. His dependence on these people scared me off from joining him. See, he's *the* Khan. He doesn't need anyone, especially not turncoats. He needs fresh blood. He needs the youth. But a lot of people are misusing his name for their own benefit. Now that he's PM, I'm hoping his party's internal accountability has improved.

As for Mian Nawaz Sharif sahib, I'm not going to get into the Panama Leaks or the other investigations that were underway against him by the time this book went to print. But there is no doubt – and my opinion here may raise quite a few eyebrows – that Mian sahib knows how to deliver.

Look at Karachi, Peshawar and Quetta, the capitals of the three provinces he's never governed. They are suffering. Look at Lahore, the province of Punjab which he governed. It's not. That's my argument.

As for the mighty Khyber Pakhtunkhwa, which is Imran Khan's territory, his party's done well there but still has a long way to go. He should follow the simple political principle of what is seen, is then sold. I want delivery for all provinces. Imran bhai hasn't gotten there yet.

So, yes. I admit it. I love Pakistani politics. I try to keep an eye on it. When I'm at home, I'm obsessed with catching the news and browsing through talk shows. Sure, they get dramatic at times. But the media is important. Pakistan matters to me. Naturally, Pakistan's politics matters too.

I know a lot of sportsmen steer clear of the potholes on the rocky road of public policy and politics. But I can't put a blindfold on and not notice and care about what needs to change. People in my position need to care. We need to give support to the needy. It is because of the people of this country that I am where I am. Yes, I enjoy my status but I refuse to live in a bubble. For the sake of the people. Politics or no politics, I will strive to work for the people of

Pakistan. That's where my foundation, the Shahid Afridi Foundation (SAF), comes in.

Of all recent leaders, I've been most impressed by General (retired) Raheel Sharif. He was one of those stand-up-and-be-counted guys. Always ready to deliver. In his historic tenure as army chief – and that *is* a controversial office in Pakistan – people went crazy for him because he made some very tough decisions. He started off with an in-house change. He cleaned up the army. Then he went for the terrorists in North Waziristan, Balochistan and Karachi. That's why he had credibility. He worked hard and made tough calls. If he wanted to run for political office, I think he would have won, hands down. Pakistanis love a good leader, be it in or out of uniform.

Towards the end of his military career, there were rumours about him staying on and getting an extension. Obviously, a public issue doesn't get more controversial than a military chief staying on in power in Pakistan. We are, after all, the land of military coups.

However, my take on the matter in 2016 wasn't something mainstream. I was of the opinion that the army must wrap up the war against terror which has been so hard-fought during these past few years, and bring it to its logical conclusion. It must finish terrorism, once and for all. If Raheel Sharif started the war, then Raheel Sharif should end it. That's what I first thought. But because his staying on would create political controversy, I was willing to shift my positioning too, based on his successor.

If the military felt that Raheel Sharif's successor was good enough to handle the war against terror as well as the mighty Pakistan army, then Sharif sahib should go ahead and retire. But if there was even an inkling of doubt about his successor, or the administration that would follow him, then Raheel Sharif must stay. That's what I'd thought when the future of the country and the army was being discussed. But thank God, General Qamar Javed Bajwa, whom I haven't met properly till date, is an able successor to lead the Pakistan army. That's because the army has a system. It's the only organization in Pakistan that has a method and sticks to it.

Back to General Raheel Sharif: meeting him was like meeting a family elder. He wanted to know about the state of Pakistan cricket, why we were not building enough cricket academies. He was hungry for information, concerned even.

Another army chief who showed the same concern for the game was General Pervez Musharraf. Sure, everybody knows that he was a big fan of cricket but I felt he was a bigger student of understanding the dynamics of improving local cricket so that it could play a role in improving Pakistan's international cricket standing. I appreciated his interest. It was a part of his statesmanship.

Unfortunately, when I met another so-called leader, I didn't get the same response. It was after one of our championship victories, when we were invited to Islamabad to meet President Asif Ali Zardari. Zardari sahib just showed up, brusquely shook our hands, smiled for the photo-op and left. He wasn't interested in our victory, in the game of cricket or in improving sports for Pakistanis. He was just counting the seconds for the photographers to do their job and leave. I was really disappointed. In fact, I remember feeling a bit angry too.

Sure, Zardari is a heck of a politician. His temperament is amazing. He survived five years in office and almost a decade in jail, a time when most people and institutions wanted his head on a stick. In a place like Pakistan, a full term in office is no small feat. Zardari is a survivor. But he isn't a cricket fan, nor is he a great leader. That's something I hold against him.

By the way, here's a little inside scoop: Qamar Javed Bajwa, the chief of army staff, does better cricket analysis than most commentators and analysts. Ramiz Raja and Harsha Bhogle, you better watch out.

33
SOLDIERING ON

MAYBE BECAUSE I generally get along with soldiers, or maybe because I always wanted to be a soldier, I'm very partial to them. If I hadn't been a cricketer, I would have been a soldier. I know it. I just do.

Maybe the influence comes from friends. Many of my closest friends have been men in uniform. Or maybe it's because of the soldiers in my family. I love the army. I love their passion for Pakistan. Nobody loves Pakistan like soldiers do. They lay their lives down for Pakistan and don't talk about it. They are the first responders in an earthquake or a flood. Their lives are disciplined. They stay within their system. They don't cross boundaries, which is the way it should be. Well, at least most of the time.

Yes, there are bad apples in the army. There are soldiers who have misused their authority. I know I'm treading into controversial territory here but I must raise the question: why, every few years, is martial law imposed in Pakistan? What's the need for the army to step in every decade or so? Why here? Why not next door?

The answer lies within our democracy and with our democrats. Our votes don't matter. There is barely any delivery of services. There is hardly any accountability. The police, the tax authorities, the people in power: do they really do justice to their mandate? Are they well led by our democratic leaders? Sorry, but the answer is no.

That's where the army comes in. That's why they have to take over. I'm pretty sure that our armed forces – the current army, not the army of the 1980s or '90s – are professional enough to not interfere in the affairs of others if there is solid governance at the centre. Only once there is a vacuum created by the democrats does the military step in. It's natural. Even the great Inzamam-ul-Haq rumbled in to bowl a few overs in matches where the bowlers were not doing their job.

I'm very partial to the General Pervez Musharraf era. Yes, he took over Pakistan's leadership in a military coup. But in the first four to five years of his rule, Pakistan did magnificently well. Its economy boomed; its media was deregulated; trade liberalization improved. But ultimately, he became more of a politician and less of a soldier – he trusted the wrong advisors and tried to play politics when he should have stayed above that stuff and concentrated on governance. If he wanted to be a leader, he needed to not act like the others. Frankly, soldiers don't know much about politics. That's a sad fact. Why they behave like politicians, I just can't say. Perhaps Imran bhai has a point when he says that our generals behave like politicians and our politicians behave like generals.

Leaders need to have a good eye. It is this eye which helps them pick a good team. It is this team that remains united as it marches towards a uniform objective. A bad eye leads to bad team selection and a bad team puts even the best leaders out of a job. In fact, a bad team destroys everything: it first turns on itself and then the system it is trying to play within.

But good leaders must have a sense of humour too. I remember visiting FATA (Federally Administered Tribal Areas, now a part of the Khyber Pakhtunkhwa province), the tribal badlands in the northwest, to inaugurate a cricket academy the army had helped me start up. General Raheel Sharif was the chief guest. I was just hanging around with him in the VIP stand and during a particularly dull phase, he asked me when the match was starting. I saw an opportunity to have some fun. I told him that the match was not starting anytime soon. General Sharif was a little startled. We were in Waziristan, after all. Not a place you can be hanging around all week. He gave me a semi-annoyed look.

So I eased in my plan and told him the match would only start once he'd face my bowling. He laughed me off. But I didn't budge. So, Raheel Sharif being Raheel Sharif said sure, why the hell not.

As we were walking up to the pitch, he told me that he was going to smash me for a four. I'm not sure whether that was a plan or an order or both. I decided it was in the nation's and my interest for the army chief to hit me for a boundary. So I bowled an unreasonably easy ball to him and he – showing no mercy – smashed me over mid-wicket for what was a remarkably powerful shot from a 56-year-old man. We both had a good laugh about it. Clips of the encounter went viral.

There's another instance of a fun moment, this time with another great soldier, General Musharraf. It was the year 2000 and we were in Lahore. Three days earlier, I had got married before a big match versus England. I did remarkably well with a five-for and a half-century. General sahib was in attendance, of course.

After the match, he came up to me and congratulated me for a job well done. Now, knowing him, he couldn't just congratulate me and decided to slip in a comment. He said something along the lines of, 'Afridi, your performance has improved after marriage.' At which point, I couldn't hold back and said, 'Well, sir, in that case,

I think I'm gonna go for a second marriage to doubly improve my performance.' We had a grand laugh and then he said that a second marriage wouldn't be a bad idea if I could score a century and get 10 wickets. Thank God, the media was not around, or the feminists would have chewed us both up for that banter.

But seriously, Musharraf sahib had the chance to fix it all during his tenure. Too bad the politicians got to him before he could change the system.

34
FUN, FANS AND FANATICS

ONE FINE day, I stopped partying. It became too much. I mean, think about it: I'm a sports star. I'm a decent-looking guy. I'm a Pathan. I'm Shahid Afridi. Obviously, things are going to happen while I'm partying, right? But I stopped it. I had to.

I enjoyed partying way too much, especially because I have a very addictive personality and I like the high of a good time (which comes naturally with the high of being a sportsman, I guess, and the constant adrenaline rush). But it's difficult to be a party animal in Pakistan. Especially the current state of Pakistan.

When we started out, there were no constraints on what we could or couldn't do. There was no social media – today, it compromises your social life. There weren't a lot of players who were religious. In fact, I started off with these superstar seniors who would kick us out of our hotel rooms, force us out, literally, and tell us to go and have some fun. As young players, we were blessed to have party animals as seniors. So, obviously, we partied. And boy, oh boy, we partied hard!

But I had to leave it. I loved it too much.

I didn't follow Imran Khan's pattern of being surrounded by superstars and socialites. But I did party, especially in my early days in the team. When I joined the team in the mid-1990s and the 2000s, we had a partying culture. Wasim bhai and Moin Khan were the leaders of the pack. We were expected to go out and not return to our rooms. It was essential, almost. Today, everybody fears the smartphone, for fear of being caught in a situation that could raise eyebrows.

I remember this one instance in Australia when we were on tour. We were in a nightclub one evening. All the guys were chatting up a girl each. I wasn't going to be left behind, so I found this real looker, a proper Melbourne girl. We chatted all night. We had a lovely evening. Upon parting, I told her I had to head to the airport in the morning to another city. She said she would come along and stay with me for the rest of the tour. Assuming she was joking, I told her, sure, why the hell not.

Guess what? She was indeed at the airport, with a ticket and all, at seven in the morning. When she came to me and said she was ready, I couldn't recognize her. Saqlain, who was my wingman the previous night, refreshed my memory, insisting that it was indeed her. I tried to dodge her throughout the check-in process. Make-up and low lights can sometimes do wonderful things to cognition.

And then there are the fans. I love my fans. I love them to bits.

But there are fans and then there are crazy fans. There are also stalkers. And then there are psychopaths. I know fangirls who travelled from villages outside Peshawar and were found in central Karachi – all in search of me. Some turned up dressed as brides at my residence. I actually had to escort them back or send for their parents to come and collect them. I've met some who've carved my name on their arms with a blade. Some women have been stalking me since 1996. A couple of them even follow me on international tours. It's quite flattering but a little crazy. And quite scary.

I remember this instance when one Sunday afternoon – my mother was still alive then – in the off season, our doorbell rang. The attendant came in and told my mother and me that some 'people' were waiting for me outside. I told him to tell the 'people' that it's a holiday and they should call and make an appointment and then come. However, my mother, God bless her soul, was shocked.

'Shahid, guests are a blessing,' she said. 'How dare you turn people away from your door?'

So, I went down to the gate to see two young women just standing there. They introduced themselves and said that there was someone in their car, parked nearby, waiting to talk to me.

I thought it was an old person or someone who couldn't leave their car, so I accompanied them to their vehicle. I peeked inside to say hello and there, in glittery red glory, sat a lovely girl dressed as an all-out bride. I still didn't get it. I figured she might be on the way to her wedding and maybe wanted to take a photograph with me or something. I congratulated her on her upcoming nuptials and she interrupted me and said, 'Shahid, I've come all the way from Peshawar. I'm ready to get married. I want to be your wife. Let's go to the mosque and get married.' Saying so, she grabbed my hand.

Besides being shocked, I was quick on my feet. I politely freed my hand and told her that while I was flattered, I was too young to get married. I thanked her and then sent her off after a few minutes of trying to convince her that she was a beautiful woman and deserved better. Phew!

Then there was this girl who would call often. This was in the '90s, when cellphones were a new thing and very expensive. So this girl started calling, totally out of the blue, and I started blowing a lot of money listening to her on the phone, giving her all the time she wanted because her voice was amazing. She sounded beautiful.

Initially, it was she who would call. Soon, I was the one who started calling her up. Remember, I wasn't married or anything at the time. So finally, I asked her to meet me. She agreed. We decided to meet on Eid in Karachi. I couldn't wait! So when Eid came, I invited her to come over and see me, as my parents would be home. It was like an arranged date!

Finally, on Eid, I couldn't keep my wits about me. The doorbell rang. I went to answer it and opened the door. There stood a young man, no more than fifteen or sixteen years old, holding a bouquet of roses. I was a little confused. So I asked him who he was. I received the shock of my life when he said he was the same 'girl' I had been talking to all these months and whom I was supposed to meet on Eid.

God! I was so embarrassed! I had said a lot of personal things to her – him – or whatever. I was also furious because I had been duped in matters of the heart! So I finally gathered the wits to ask him why he had pretended to be a woman and he said that he'd heard that I only talk to girls on the phone and not men! I was so embarrassed! I didn't know whether to give him a whipping or invite him in for a cup of tea.

I did the latter and made small talk, not being able to maintain eye contact with this young lad. Eventually, I warmed up to him as I came up with another bright idea: I would deploy him for the same trick he had played on me – with my friends.

So I started using him to play pranks on my pals. He duped quite a few of them, just like he had duped me. God, he had a gorgeous voice. Very versatile! He could even sing in the voice of a woman. He would invite my pals over for a date and stand them up. He had quite a wicked sense of humour. Will you believe it, he even convinced a pal of mine – a famous bowler I won't name – over the phone to marry him?

I like gigs outside of cricket. I like doing ads. It's fun working with the camera. But the Pakistani ad-makers have a very different approach compared to international ad filmmakers: they have no respect for time and even the smallest job takes days. The *goras*, on the other hand, are more punctual.

But I've liked working in front of the camera. In the beginning, it was tough. You eventually get used to it. The lone shoots aren't fun. It's good to have some company, some partners around. I remember doing this soft drink ad with the boys, back in the day. Wasim Akram, Javed Miandad and the gang were in it. The problem was, Javed had to say a line, and he couldn't deliver it properly because of his lisp. We were there for two hours, all for Javed's one-liner, which was: 'Humain jazbay ke saath khelna hai'. Only problem was, he kept on saying, 'Humain zuzbay ke saath khelna hai'. It was hilarious. Poor guy.

As for celebrity crushes, I wish I had one. I believe most celebrities are made up. Too much make-up, literally, if you know what I mean. If you want to be a serious cricketer, you have to leave your weaknesses behind. You've got to be a serious professional. And, these days, you've got to do yourself a favour and stay away from social media as much as possible. Some of my recent tweets have received more attention than was required. I'm learning from this experience.

I've advised the young guns in the team – especially the ones who start feeling the love and hype of social media after a good performance – to keep some distance from it. It's destructive. It builds you up, makes you a star and then rips you apart. One bad performance and all the insults and trolling which come your way shatter your nerves and confidence. You can't take the pressure. In effect, you become a victim of your own social media machine. It's bad for business.

Eventually, when you've developed a thick skin, you should be able to do your own thing. But the replacement of old-school partying and socializing with the tempting, addictive world of social media gimmickry is ridiculous. It's made lesser men of sportsmen. It's got to go.

35
A TARDY ENDING

IT WASN'T easy playing cricket. Nor was it easy leaving it.

I still remember the exact moment when it became clear that I was done.

We were in Adelaide, during the 2015 World Cup quarter-final against world champs Australia. Our scoreline wasn't reading too well. At 124 for 5, Umar Akmal had just been caught at mid-wicket attempting a lazy shot. Misbah-ul-Haq had been dismissed before him, caught at the same spot, by the same fielder. It seemed like almost everybody in the team was falling to outfield catching throughout the tournament. We weren't learning from our mistakes, collectively.

I walked out. My last seven innings against the Aussies, starting from 2010, had been 1, 2, 0, 7, 5, 2 and 6. Something bigger was needed.

I would try, but not really make a difference. With 24 runs off 15 balls, I would fire, then misfire, then miscue. Aaron Finch would catch me, near the boundary, off Josh Hazlewood.

My last shot in ODI cricket would be a pull. Maybe because I hadn't pushed myself enough. It wasn't a very glorious exit, not after 398 ODIs.

We would go on to fight with the ball. Wahab Riaz would bowl one of the most memorable spells in modern cricket, almost taking Shane Watson's head off a few times. After he would tire out, Australia would take over and then grab the World Cup too.

In Tests, I would be in and out of love, wrapping things up by 2006 and then making a begrudged start-and-stop in 2010. Tests weren't even for me. But if the stats are to be believed, I was made for Tests. The T20s – I would continue to play them till the World T20 in 2016, and then further on, the PSL and other leagues would be more my type of cricket; but that would be more entertainment than proper cricket, really. By 2017–18, I would even graduate to T10s. Hell, I'm going to be playing T5s at 60, if I ever get there.

But ODIs were and remain my first love. I debuted in an ODI. I would essentially end my career in one. My 37-ball century against Sri Lanka was a record that stood for 17 years till Corey Anderson broke it (100 off 36 balls) against the West Indies in January 2014.

There was some clarity the day I heard about Anderson breaking my Nairobi record. A year later, when I heard that AB de Villiers had broken Anderson's record – 100 not out off 31 balls, also against West Indies – the writing on the wall was stark and clear: my time was up. A new generation of players was at the helm. All that was left for me was a formal exit.

In retrospect, that's what the ICC 2015 World Cup and the World T20 in 2016 became for me: exit points. We live large lives; at least some of us do. But only some become larger than life. Not all of us get to pick when to say goodbye.

Take Sachin Tendulkar. He had, in my opinion, the perfect exit. He beat us fair and square in Mohali and then his team destroyed Sri Lanka to lift the World Cup in 2011, in his hometown, Mumbai. What a glorious career! What a perfect ending!

And then, there are the lesser mortals, who are edged out not by our choice, but by time and space.

This is a good moment to look back.

For someone who was brought into the team as a bowler, my batting became everything. Perhaps this was unfair, even unwise. The spectacle evolved. The fans proliferated. The crowds grew. The cameos unravelled. So did the frustrations and politics of the dressing room.

Then, a decade later, my bowling became essential. The quicker one. The googlies. The fast over rates. It's this very bowling that would peak in 2011, when I led Pakistan to the 2011 World Cup, got more scalps than anybody else but did not survive the death match versus India.

Yet, it was my batting that remained a question mark. It would make a mark in the shortest format indelibly. T20 would become my thing, but not for long. The World T20 in 2007 would be exciting but evasive. I would get Man of the Tournament, but not the crown. Still, in 2009, I would get a chance to stand and deliver: catching Scott Styris would change the tournament for us. It would change me. I was a different player against South Africa in the semis and against Sri Lanka in the final. But frankly, it had taken that horrific attack against the Lankans in Lahore and the death of international cricket in Pakistan to help me make sense of the whole thing, even myself.

I walked into trouble too – booting the pitch against England in 2005, eating the ball in Australia in 2010, taking on the PCB every few years and taking the coach head-on every few months. I was belligerent. I could have improved on that front, too.

But every time I would be banned or kicked out, I'd bounce back. Harder. Faster. Bigger. But eventually, I would stop getting better. There would be moments – like the 7 for 12 and the 76 against West Indies in 2013, and the Asia Cup in 2014. But by the time 2015 would roll around, I would be done. Almost done, till that will-we-or-will-we-not World T20 started in India in 2016.

What a disaster, eh? A proper one. Made in Pakistan, unfolded in India. The perfect storm.

Time for a brutal assessment. Bad decisions held us back in that tournament, my last one on the global stage. Bad selection held us back, too. For example, I wanted to drop a fast bowler and play Imad Wasim in the match against India at Kolkata. We needed a spinner. But Wiqi bhai and Intikhab Alam sahib wanted things their way.

I knew what could happen with all this lack of coordination and trust. Before that last trip to India, I had made a public disclaimer, which went viral and blazed through the press, that things weren't going to go well for us. I tried to play it down, and was serious about the need to get our house in order before we went over to the other side. Nobody bothered to listen.

But as we say in my language: it's not that the knife is sharp; it is your stomach that's weak.

Our thinking is limited. Pakistanis compete with each other more than they compete with outsiders. This may be our biggest failing as a nation. Our insecurities get the better of us. It's always about X Pakistani batsman saying I played better than Y Pakistani batsman. Pakistani bowler A wants to be faster than Pakistani bowler B. He doesn't want to scalp AB de Villiers or rip apart Virat Kohli – which, by the way, is his real job. There's a team within the team. And it's captained by self-interest and petty politics.

What went wrong in the 2016 World T20? We made a strong start but after losing to India, we just kept on losing. I tried to do what I could individually but towards the end, I must admit that I wasn't in control of my team. It was every man for himself, really. That's exactly what seemed to be happening on the field, and publicly too.

Frankly, we were out of form. New talent wasn't emerging (I had openly displayed my concern about that too, and have explained it earlier in detail). There was a chronic shortage of fresh blood. And the guys who were coming into the team, well, I didn't feel the fire in their bellies. They were giving up easily. They were soft. That's not cricket. It's definitely not Pakistan cricket.

In the buildup to my retirement in 2016, a lot changed. There was a lot on my mind when I decided to hang up my boots and walk away. Just before the World T20 in India, I wanted to quit for good. My performance wasn't up to par. I was failing consistently in terms of my own performances. So was the team. If the team would have reached the semis or even the final, then at least I would have looked good on my way out.

Sounds egomaniacal? Yes. I wanted to leave on a high note. Can you blame me? After 20 years of international cricket, wouldn't you want a glorious exit? But even quitting hasn't been easy for me. There was a lot that was off-kilter. We were not looking solid as a unit for years, particularly since the spot-fixing controversy. Even friends who had been there and done that came in with advice which unfortunately backfired.

For example, I asked Imran Khan to come and see the boys before the India game at the World T20. That meeting turned into something else, a total disaster, really. First, we waited for him for hours so he could come and say something inspiring. Unfortunately, when he did arrive, the pep talk turned into a therapy session for some of the team members. Umar Akmal even complained about his place in the batting order. How juvenile! So instead of preparing us mentally to play India, Imran went on to wax eloquent about the bloody methodology of the batting order. What a wasted opportunity!

What's more, when Imran returned to Pakistan, he fired a missile – he claimed the team was under pressure and we couldn't handle the situation in India[1]. It was a real disaster. As for Akmal, or all those who I have played with or against, any player who seeks soft corners or makes excuses isn't really a player. He's a

---

[1] Press Trust of India, 'Absorbing pressure, not pep talks, wins matches: Imran on Pak loss', *Hindustan Times*, March 21, 2016.

supplicant. He's just doing a job, not playing the game. He can't take the pressure. Umar Akmal could not. Sorry buddy, but that's what I really feel.

So that is the context of what was going on in the team before it was curtains for me in 2016. Yet, I wasn't all there, be it on the field or off it. That's why I decided I would take a final call on arriving back in Pakistan. Sometimes, home offers you more than just comfort. It offers you a chance to introspect. I needed closure.

It was a tough spot to be in. The problem was, I had already announced that I wanted to retire. But people I trusted were of the opinion that I needed to give league cricket and T20s another shot.

Meanwhile, at the PCB, there was a reshuffle in the works. Inzi bhai was the new chief selector. There was a new captain – the hard-working Sarfaraz Ahmed – in place. The media brought out its fangs, ripping into the old guard and gunning for new players. There was a whole new outlook which was being introduced in the team. Would I fit in? Tough question. But God bless Inzi bhai for giving me the option of doing whatever I wanted. He told me, 'We will do whatever works for you. You're in the driver's seat. You decide.'

To hear this from a selector was really a big deal. I've played most of my cricket under Inzi bhai. He's one heck of a cricketer. He's almost always kept his cool (that walk-off in England was not one of those moments). And he's only gotten wiser over the years.

That's where we came up with a great solution to what was brewing into a controversy around my retirement: I would play a farewell T20 match against the West Indies in the UAE.

The reasoning was simple. Inzi and I were both in agreement that Pakistani cricket, while great in tradition, lacked the ability to honour its best. Farewells are non-events. Players come. Players play. And then they either wither away or are kicked out unceremoniously (usually it's the latter). Unfortunately, that's the Pakistani nature of send-offs. And not just in cricket.

Inzi bhai and I also agreed that instead of an inglorious exit, why couldn't we start a new tradition? That's when he took the idea of a farewell match to the PCB. The chairman, Shehryar Khan sahib, was hospitalized at the time, so Inzi bhai took it to the COO, Subhan Ahmad. And, of course, Subhan Ahmad being Subhan Ahmad, took it to the press.

I was really disturbed by this development. All I'd wanted was to set a new precedent – a new tradition of honouring our sportsmen. In other countries, when a cricketer retires, prime ministers come and see off a player for his final farewell game. What's the big deal, I thought, if there was a ceremony or something to send me off?

The issue, really, was Najam Sethi. The new co-chairman – that's what his position essentially was – felt that he wasn't looped into this conversation. (This was the internal narrative of the PCB.) Thus, the matter was needlessly politicized. Instead, the story that began doing the rounds was that I was gunning for a custom-made farewell match especially designed for me to be featured in. Naturally, it made the wrong impression on the media, who obviously jumped on it.

You see, with Najam Sethi sahib it's rather clear. At the time, the PCB was in a particularly bizarre stage of its rather bizarre history: it had two chairpersons. Najam Sethi sahib may have been president of the board at the time but the decision-making in such matters was more of a 50:50 thing between him and Shehryar Khan. That's the way most Pakistani organizations are managed – or mismanaged, if you prefer. We divide and get conquered.

As for Sethi, well, I don't have any problems with the man, despite his political connections with – and appointment by – the Nawaz Sharif regime. Also, credit should be given where it's due. He has done a great job of growing the PSL and getting the zing in cricket back to Pakistan. The PSL is here to stay. At a time when the project was at a standstill, when it had no takers, he made things happen. Good for him and good for cricket.

But ego is a dangerous thing. And this is why I must recall what he did to me in my last days in the Pakistan team.

As I mentioned earlier, the decision around my last match became needlessly controversial and blown out of proportion. When Subhan Ahmad – also our media manager – took my conversation with Inzi to the media, Najam Sethi read about it in the papers and began doubting our intentions. Soon, the coach – Waqar Younis – got involved. It all got very ugly. To solve the issue, Sethi said there was going to be no such farewell match and offered me an award and money instead.

I never wanted either. I just wanted to run a lap around the ground and thank people. That's it. But Sethi wanted me to accept the award money from him, in person. I refused. He eventually relented and okayed the farewell game. But it was embarrassing that he gave the award money to a charity of his choice, not my choice (Shahid Afridi Foundation). Unbelievable.

And here's something even more unbelievable. When Misbah-ul-Haq and I were doing our final goodbyes at the ground, Najam Sethi never bothered leaving his office for a minute to come over to the outfield to participate in the farewell. With the whole world watching Pakistan's Test captain, Misbah, and your humble all-rounder exit after twenty years, the cricket boss of the country never bothered to offer even a public handshake. Amazing.

Today, I hope there's no political baggage or bad blood between us. But during that controversy around the so-called farewell match, Sethi versus Afridi became an ego match instead.

To repeat: all I wanted to do was set a good precedent. That's all. I always was Shahid Afridi, am Shahid Afridi and will remain Shahid Afridi. A farewell match was never going to be the making or breaking of me. I wanted to create a new tradition. And I didn't beg for one just for myself.

I know I wasn't the perfect player, the greatest captain or the best man in the field.

The papers would say that my 'death or glory' approach was my downfall. They got it wrong, right from day one. They never understood that I was a spinner who could also bat on the side. They never understood that my temperament issue – which ran for years – was based on meeting those expectations set on that first day in Nairobi.

They didn't understand a lot.

And so, confused, lost and out of focus, I finished my international career in stages. Just 27 Tests, scoring 1,176 runs with a highest score of 156 and 48 wickets; 398 ODIs with 8,064 runs, a highest score of 124 while taking 395 wickets. And 99 T20I matches with 1,405 runs and 98 wickets.

But those are just numbers. And numbers don't matter. *Niyat* does.

36

HAPPINESS, FAITH AND DOUBT

POTENTIAL HAS to be harnessed. Unfortunately, mine wasn't.

I don't think I was treated and groomed the way I should have been. Coaches and captains didn't exploit my talent to the fullest. I was misused. Not deployed properly, nor unleashed. There is a whole roster of coaches, especially Pakistani coaches, who wanted me to play the way they had played the game. They wanted to recreate me as a reflection of their own image. This created in me the biggest defect a cricketer can have: doubt.

I became double-minded. Confused, really. There was an entire phase in my career where I would take to the pitch but couldn't deliver the way I should have. I wasn't myself. I feared staying on the pitch because I felt I wasn't really meant to be there. I feared heading back to the dressing room because of my fear of getting out. If I bungled the innings, got out, or didn't bat like I was supposed to, or if I let the coach down, it would scare the hell out of me and haunt my game. This happened with a number of coaches, over the years. The vicious circle of doubt kept getting bigger.

Then came a tipping point: Bob Woolmer, the only coach who let me play like I wanted to play. Just like the way I was born to play. He told me to just be myself. I stopped worrying how much cricket there was left in me and went back to playing the way I always wanted to.

And then there was the bowling, which, I must repeat, is what I was really born to do, and given the national cap for. I had a healthy rivalry with Saqlain Mushtaq, the wily off-spinner. He was a death overs specialist. He would wrap up the tail like it was an Eid gift. He loved doing it.

I remember, once Saqlain and I got into a debate. I goaded him into an argument which stood statistically, telling him he could only deal with tail-enders, while most of my wickets were of top- and middle-order batsmen. He bet wrongly. We went to the team stats guru and guess what – about 60 per cent of Saqlain's wickets were indeed tail-enders. Meanwhile, about 70 per cent of my wickets were top- and middle-order batsmen.

Unfortunately, I wasn't developed as a bowler, especially in the early years. I was never given the whole 10-over deal. Yes, I was known – and still am – for my breakthrough spells. I remember getting Sachin out a few times. I also fondly recall dismissing Ricky Ponting quite a few times. There was a seven-wicket haul I got against the Windies. I was the highest wicket-taker in the 2011 World Cup. By the late 2000s, I eventually transitioned to being a better bowler than a batsman. But bowling is all about rhythm. And in the early years, neither my coaches nor my skippers trusted me to bloom into a full-time bowler. That's a pity because I was called into the Pakistan team as a bowler who could bat too – not the other way around.

Have you heard about the all-rounder's conundrum? No? Try it on for size: what feels better – hitting the world's most dangerous bowler for a six or dislocating the middle stump of the planet's finest batsman? Tough question, eh? That's what you call the all-rounder's conundrum.

In my case, what's my bigger fantasy? Hitting McGrath for a six or getting Ponting out? Well, neither really, because I did both and did them enough. But the answer, frankly, is that both made me happy as hell – a different kind of happy. I've always wondered whether I'm happier smacking the ball out of the park or dismissing big batsmen home to their wives. Honestly, I think it depends on the moment.

You have to see the moment coming, though. At least, you should try to. Forget the fleeting moment of the crucial dismissal, or the match-winning six. Let's talk about the big one. Let's talk about marriage.

I had an arranged marriage. I lived my bachelor years to the fullest. I made a lot of friends, enjoyed a very active social life and partied hard. But when it came to marriage, I trusted my parents with making the right choice. It's the way things are with our family.

It started with my dad. One evening, he summoned me to the terrace to speak to me in private. When I went to him, he announced very nonchalantly that I had been engaged to be married. I didn't think twice, nor did I ask any questions. I just said, 'That's great news, Baba!' My father was actually surprised. He was expecting me to question him and the decision he'd made for me. Maybe because I was *that* son, the one who was the outlier to the family's narrative about jobs and stability. But I did not. And he loved me for it. I remember his eyes teared up that moment as he hugged me.

I loved my parents equally and it was tough losing them both. They departed at different times. My father struggled for years – seven to be precise – with cancer. I was more prepared for his passing away. I was older too. But the way I lost my mother hurt more. She had just said her afternoon prayer and was settling down to take a nap with her prayer beads. She lay down, and never woke up. Her prayer beads were still in her hands. She was 52 years old. At the time, I was maybe 20 or 21 years old. I remember, she would pray that she never become a burden on any of us during old age. Maybe, her prayers were heard and she left us too soon. That afternoon, when she passed away, my life paused and things came to a standstill for quite a while. It was a difficult time.

But with loss, God also teaches you patience. After my mother's death, I started touring more. I found form. I recovered. But I never moved on. I don't think I'm over her loss, even now. I was more prepared when Baba left us. Not when she did.

Our *qismet* is in our hands. There is even a *hadith* about how we can change our fate. We can change it all if we want. But in my culture, they say that women bring their own luck to the family. Things changed for the better when I got married. Over the years, I became father to four daughters – Aqsa, Ajwa, Asmara and Ansha. Truth be told, with the birth of each, my luck kept on improving. Daughters are a blessing. They really are.

Aqsa is in the 10th grade, Ansha is in the ninth. They're both great at sports and even better in academics. Ansha wants to help out with the Shahid Afridi Foundation after she completes her studies. Ajwa and Asmara are the youngest and love to play dress-up. They have my permission to play any sport, as long as they're indoors. Cricket? No, not for my girls. They have permission to play all the indoor games they want, but my daughters are not going to be competing in public sporting activities. It's for social and religious reasons that I've made this decision and their mother agrees with me. The feminists can say what they want; as a conservative Pakistani father, I've made my decision.

I've always given religion a place in my heart. It started with my family. I started praying very early in life. I found solace in it. Today, it is an important part of my parenting regime as well. It doesn't matter what sort of day I've had. When I pray, everything makes sense. Everything. Whenever I miss my morning prayers, I have a terribly stressful day. The day I hit all my targets must include my praying five times a day.

I try to keep the family together. My sisters. My brothers. My cousins. Whenever I'm in Karachi, I try to have them over once a

week. They all come over and get together and I do what I can to help
them out and fix their problems. And then we eat. Together.

I've been lucky. I haven't seen abject poverty. We got close to it,
sure, but we had a smart father who always set things right when
they got rough. Before we moved to Karachi from Khyber, my father
made sure we had a proper place for us to live, with a secure roof
over our heads.

Soon after we all arrived in Karachi, my father had enough to
make us a little house. We weren't terribly rich, though. But we were
fortunate and there was *barkat*, blessings and goodwill, in what we
earned. We had a modest income. We lived within our means. We
had enough to last the month but not beyond that. It wasn't much
but it was good enough. Of course, it wasn't easy. Not by any means.
I think that lifestyle gave me a can-do ethic, which is hinged on my
belief that things eventually work out. Self-belief is key, but things
indeed tend to work themselves out. Yes, there were setbacks along
the way. But we overcame them.

Of course, I have fears. I have sinned. Who hasn't? But if you've
done good deeds, you don't even fear death. But you know what
really scares me? The world that awaits the younger generation. My
kids. Your kids. The unregulated exposure of the internet, with our
kids in the mix. That is what scares me.

Different people have different fears. For example, I've read, heard
and even seen that Imran Khan is scared to fail. It's a reason for his
success. He can't handle failure. But for me, failure is an opportunity.
You can always bounce back. You can trip, you can fall, but you have
to get back on your feet again. You cannot, ever, give up. I've been
kicked out of teams. I've been injured, I've been politically written
off. I've even been picked at. But I haven't stopped.

Moreover, I don't care whether you're a believer or not and it
doesn't matter if you're a Muslim or a Hindu or an atheist or whatever,
hard work is always rewarded. If you believe in God, He does the
rewarding. If you don't believe in Him – though you should – life

rewards you. The universe rewards you. Good deeds bring good gains. That's what I think.

It's a funny thing, fortune. Some people have a lot of it in a good way, while others don't. I don't think I was deserving of all that I've received. Allah has given me more than I deserve. I don't think I was good enough to have what He has given me, really.

But there is a fire in me to do more, to achieve more. There is more in me than just cricket. Once you start achieving your objectives and tasting success, your bigger goals become clearer. Your family's expectations increase even more. You get into this no-fail zone. You don't fail because you can't fail. It's cosmic, rewarding, crazy stuff. And karma? It exists.

Maybe honour has a lot do with achievement. You want to leave behind a legacy. For example, with the Shahid Afridi Foundation, I want honesty and hard work to be attached to my name even after I'm gone. You want your legacy to last, don't you?

You worry about the future? That's why you must work hard today. You really should.

37
THE SECOND INNINGS

O N 16 December 2014, six Pakistani Taliban gunmen entered the
Army Public School in Peshawar and conducted what would
become one of the deadliest massacres of all time. One hundred and
forty-nine people were killed, of which 132 were schoolchildren aged
between eight and 18. Eventually, the Pakistani military forces would
launch an operation and kill the gunmen, but by then Pakistan would
be a different country.

I wasn't in Pakistan at the time but what I started seeing on
WhatsApp about the attacks was disturbing. I didn't want to believe
it. None of it. It felt like these were photos and clips from Syria or
Afghanistan, not Pakistan. I didn't want to believe it and indeed, I
could not believe it.

But there's always a silver lining. Even in the death of over 100
kids. The incident woke up our nation. The National Action Plan
was drafted. The opposition and the government got their house
in order. The army got clear directives about the end goal: wipe
out terrorism. It woke us up, even those among us who were on
the fence.

I'm disappointed with our political leadership, though. Politics is a business in Pakistan. The leadership is not the kind of national leadership meant to inspire. It's all about partisan, vested, limited or personal interests. There is no long-term plan for the country. There is no national vision to fight crime. There is no common policy to tackle joblessness. There is not a single page, nor a proposal on how we can improve our national pastime and love: cricket.

Our politicians, insecure that they are, try to grab what they can in the few years they get in office. Achieving public office is not to retain the public's trust but the public's wealth. Most of them are there to plunder wealth.

As for the army, I'm afraid they don't have any idea about politics. They know a lot about politicians but they don't know politics. This is a fact. Their coming to power is always to fill a vacuum. It's a desperate move. But soon, even they start playing political games and thus become dependent on corrupt politicians. That's when things start going downhill for the country.

General Pervez Musharraf, former president of Pakistan, is the perfect example of this. He got consumed by his own ambitions and instead of concentrating on changes, started playing politics. Pakistan needs a national think-tank of 40–50 of our finest: soldiers, politicians, business leaders, intellectuals, who should give the government advice and the government should take it seriously. And the government should always be run by civilians – honourable ones. Those are my two cents.

I have no political ambitions. Actually, that's not true. At the moment, I do not have political ambitions. I'm quite a serious fan of politics – I see it as a public service – but I don't think there's one, not one, political party that I can join at the moment. And frankly, if I try to create my own party, I will probably be kicked out by my party members. I'm terribly naïve.

About Mian Nawaz Sharif: he's a good guy. Once upon a time, I was actually very fond of him. He's a got a big heart. But he didn't learn much from all his time in and out of politics. His social media approach of late has been disastrous and has been divisive for Pakistan. He didn't use his fan following for the country or even his party. He used it all for himself. That's just wrong. And when he was being tried, he made it all about himself, not the country.

You know what a good leader does when in power? He reaches out to everyone. He asks the opposition for help and advice about how to improve things. He even goes and talks to the state's enemies if he has to. He doesn't shut them out. He doesn't shoo them off. If you've got millions of votes, you should have the confidence to work with people across parties and institutions. If you're really serious about running Pakistan, you need to work with the whole country.

It's sad – the whole political circus is a scam. The *jalsas*, the glitzy political rallies, are attended by the types who don't vote. Meanwhile, on polling day the votes go to the machines which have been running the country into the ground. So we end up with a government which behaves like Turkish leader Recep Tayyab Erdoğan's, without any populist support. But with the 2018 elections and Imran Khan's advent, we've seen that change somewhat. I'm not sure if it's going to be sustainable.

You know what our greatest tragedy is? The lack of education. We don't read. We don't process. We don't analyse. We are not accountable. Consequently, our leaders just play politics, not serve the people. And you know who is to blame the most for this? Us. The so-called haves, not the have-nots.

Here's the truth about the wealth gap: the have-nots, whether in Pakistan or India or elsewhere, unfortunately, are as downtrodden and as uneducated as the have-nots anywhere else in the world. Poverty is a global issue. All poor people starve, all poor people are helpless, wherever they may be.

However, the haves – the elites, the powerful, the successful – are the ones who should be questioned for what ails us. They hold power. They call the shots. Most 'extremists' are poor. Most people who cultivate, politicize and exploit this extremism are rich.

I don't mean to sound like a socialist but Pakistan's elite lack the spine, patience and wherewithal to deal with the country. They run traffic lights in their crore-rupee cars. If they can't wait for a light to turn green, even with their Harvard and Oxford degrees, how can they expect regular folk to abide by the law? That's the tragedy of Pakistan. Nobody fixes the basics. Everyone just talks big and thinks small.

I've been blamed for being partisan. They said I took sides when I helped Imran Khan's government in their education initiative. That's wrong. I wasn't supporting Khan. I was supporting the people. I did the same for polio vaccination. When the military was fighting to secure polio workers (who were being attacked in droves), I wasn't supporting the army. I was supporting polio workers. Why shouldn't I? My origins are from amongst the people. The people of my country are my strength. They are my only interest. I will rise and fall with the people. That's why the Shahid Afridi Foundation is getting into everything – hospitals, water treatment plants, schools, even microfinance. Whatever I can do, I will do. Public service is the future for me.

I can't say what's next. I have a political bug, that's for sure. Yes, as clichéd as it sounds for many cricketers in South Asia, there is a political animal in me, but I will be the first to admit that I'm probably not cut out for contemporary local or national politics in Pakistan. Elders and mentors don't recommend it for me either. They are probably right.

Pakistani politics – or politics anywhere in the world – is a dirty business full of U-turns, lies, hypocrisy and insults. I don't think I'm looking forward to a future where I appear on some talk show and lie to millions just because that's the need of the job or the requirement of my political party. So, unless the nature of politics changes in Pakistan – a far shot, for I assume it's the same elsewhere too – I know I'm not naturally cut out to be a politician. If my elders advise otherwise, I may think about it.

As for social work, of course, I will never stop helping. The hospital I've made in Taghibanda, my birthplace in Khyber, will only grow. It used to be a 10-bed set-up but now we have expanded and have two more wards in there, including one labour room for mothers-to-be. I'm also planning to try out similar projects all over the country but focusing on underdeveloped areas at first. My approach is to first build small achievable projects without the hype. Not the huge national controversies that many 'celebrity projects' end up becoming. Even something as modest as a couple of rooms can function as a little medical clinic or a hospital as long as it's located in the right area and has the required facilities.

So, admittedly, I think I have these two bugs: politics and social work. But they both come from the same ambition: helping those who are in need. If it's politically possible, without the lies and the insulting, sure, I will do it politically. If I have to become a social worker, that's what I will do. But my ambition is to help others. It's how I always treated my teammates and it's how I want to treat the rest of my country.

I've been asked if I'd like to consider a future as a cricket coach. Honestly, I don't have the temperament for it. I may begin explaining something to a young lad and even attempt it a second time. But by the third attempt, if he doesn't get it, I'd probably end up slapping him. Okay, maybe I'm exaggerating (for the record, I've never struck a junior player) but I wasn't coddled or spoonfed my cricket – I don't know how to do it to another either. Modern coaching is about coddling. And coddling is for boys, not men.

So, coaching at the international level is out of the question. I know a lot of other guys in the team who have such ambitions – coaching a foreign team and living on the global circuit. Why, I wonder. Why not apply your great skills to help out local kids who need it the most at the U-14 level? Or coach the guys who are about to get a break and be 'discovered' at the U-19 level? Don't they need mentors? Don't they need an international star on their side to teach them how to excel and earn their spurs? That's the kind of mentoring and guidance that will make them international cricketers one day. That's the kind of cricketing ecosystem that will sustain Pakistan cricket in the future.

It is in this spirit that I want to make a cricket academy in the northwestern tribal areas, in my home of FATA, which have some of the strongest and most talented kids in the country but, unfortunately, they haven't been able to tap into the mainstream cricket system because of the long-drawn conflict in the region. That's why, if the PCB wants me to, I'd love to do something to strengthen domestic cricket. But I wouldn't do it on the traditional bureaucratic terms, or by being the board's yes-man. I'd do my bit independently only and with the understanding that I have full freedom to make and implement domestic cricket policies. After all, that is the need of the hour.

As for the cricket, I think I will continue till I hang up my boots. The 20-over format has encouraged a 10-over format. And the day is not far when the 10-over format's success will introduce the five-over format.

Despite all my anger about what's wrong with my country and those who run it, I'm bullish about Pakistan. Good things are happening here. Great things, in fact.

My parents' prayers got me to where I am today. Sure, my own hard work helped a little. But the fact that I never had ill intentions for anyone was key. That's how I got to where I am. I help out whomever I can. These are my foundational traits. God helps me because of these traits. The rest, only He knows.

As for the reception to my game even now – people rising to their feet when I make my way, padded up, to the middle, and leaving the stadium when I'm dismissed – and the whole star-power value, well, it's aggression, passion and emotion that make a star. Not just a performance, but a *pyaar* to play, with the right *niyat*.

Yes, I'm a game changer. I changed the way things were done in this great game.

But I'm not a cricketer. I'm simply a player. I love to play. I love to have fun. And I've considered it a privilege and an honour to have entertained millions, not just my fellow countrymen, along the way.

38
NAYA PAKISTAN, PURANA LALA

ICOULDN'T vote in 2018. I tried to make my schedules work but couldn't make it back to Pakistan in time. I regret missing out.

The 2018 elections in Pakistan were a landmark one. A cricketer is now the prime minister of the world's sixth most populous country. Unfortunately, these elections came with some serious baggage. A narrative that continues to do the rounds is that the polls were not fair. I feel the jury is out on that one: it was a 50:50 thing.

But here's a fact: Imran Khan is now the elected prime minister of Pakistan. We have to give him the respect that a prime minister deserves. We have to make things work.

That's where the media comes in. The role of the media will be essential in the coming years. For the sake of the future of Pakistan, the media must pull up its socks. It must ensure that our local governance is in order, that the government is accountable to the people of the Pakistan and that our reputation, globally, improves for the right reasons.

As for his vision, I don't have any doubts about Imran's integrity or the goals he has set to achieve – a vision that he calls 'Naya Pakistan', the new Pakistan.

The real question which bothers me, though, is his team selection. Sure, he has read the pitch, but is Imran doing what he was most famous for on the cricket field – putting the right man in the right job?

If he succeeds, his goals are so lofty that no doubt he will turn Pakistan's fortunes around. But the way I'm seeing things develop, he's restarting things from scratch. He's putting a lot of pressure on himself. He's on a long-term timeline. From debt to corruption – our two main challenges – he's got a revolutionary but a difficult-to-implement plan.

No doubt, he has created a new self-awareness in Pakistan's polity. I know, commenting about the prime minister is easier said than done. But there's no doubt in my mind that Khan's *niyat*, intention, is fine. His ability to execute – rather, his team's ability – is what bothers me.

I'm a big fan of what Khan's Naya Pakistan is doing with India. From his peace overtures (I quote his first speech, about Pakistan taking two steps towards peace if the Indians take one step – an approach I personally believe in too) to opening the Kartarpur corridor and releasing the Indian Air Force pilot shot down by the Pakistanis in February 2019 – peaceful relations with India are essential. Both countries, even the subcontinental region, will flourish.

However, Imran Khan must do more about Kashmir. We have to resolve that issue. We have to save the Kashmiri people, and we must involve them in the peace process. Nobody in the Indian subcontinent has suffered or struggled more than Kashmiris. So much resources go into guarding this territory. So much goes into policing the Line of Control. So many mouths can get fed, so many minds can be nourished, if India and Pakistan resolve the Kashmir issue through a Kashmiri-owned, Kashmiri-led peace process.

By the way, my bit in London last year about Kashmir – I mentioned that Pakistan must first clean its house first before it tries to liberate Kashmir – was totally taken out of context. I got emotional about the issue. My timing could have been better too.

But you heard it from me: Kashmir belongs to the Kashmiris. Not to Indians. Not to Pakistanis. That debate comes later. But first and foremost, Kashmir is for the Kashmiri people themselves.

These are interesting times. Pakistan stands at the cusp of so much – internally and internationally. But the question about changing this place and turning it around haunts me. How can one be a Pakistani, especially an influential Pakistani, and not want to improve this country? How can you drive around the streets of Pakistan, see what's around you and still not want to change it?

I must say something for the record here. It might make people angry but it must be said. Whatever facilities the military gets in Pakistan, the police and other civil services must get the same. The same academies, the same training facilities, the same resources must be given to all. That's the only way the service delivery and law and order will improve in this country.

Thus, the civil–military imbalance must be fixed. The army, as the more powerful institution, must take the lead here. It must lend its best and brightest to all institutions, or it must share its best practices with others. It cannot exist in isolation. Moreover, we must all think long term – from the cricket, to peace with India, to education, to birth control and health, we must think only for the long term. Too many short-term shortcuts have been taken in this land. It's time to change that.

By the time this book is published, the Afghan peace process may have led to something. The region may have stabilized. Finally, the Americans are thinking straight, engaged in a formal peace process. If one is serious about peace in Afghanistan, one must understand that you cannot beat the Taliban. Their Pashtun blood will not let them rest. You must engage them politically. I'm glad the long war maybe, finally, coming to an end.

But Indo–Pak peace? That's a whole different argument and boils down to one man: Narendra Modi.

As long as Modi is around, I'm not sure if there will ever be peace with Pakistan. Khan sahib, clearly, is relatively more flexible than Modi ji. He has already proven this.

Also, as I've said earlier, Modi is no Vajpayee. Modi has polarized his country. I worry for India under him. But, no matter if you like him or not, peace in the region depends on Modi. He is an important man. If he does contribute to peace, there's no doubt that millions of impoverished people will praise him forever. They need peace the most.

Some free advice for anyone gunning for peace in the subcontinent: use cricket. It's the only element that can get us to sit on the same table. Use the sport wisely. The greatest game in the world can build the greatest nations on this planet. Think about that.

And remember: always pad up. You never know when you might get sent in to bat.

Change the game. But first, change yourself.

Cricket Zindabad. Pakistan Paindabad.

INDEX

Index

Index

Index

ACKNOWLEDGEMENTS

THIS BOOK took longer than it was supposed to.

We are tortured souls, Shahid and I, with bad schedules, attention deficits and connectivity issues, both technical and emotional. Not only did we have to drop the mask and really learn how to talk to each other with honesty, but we also needed the encouragement to keep going.

My beautiful, all-knowing wife, Shaan Ali Khan, the mother of my two lovely girls but also the brains behind this outfit and the sage of this book, was the actual driver of this operation. Had she not pushed Shahid and me to stay connected, and constantly encouraged me to write, we wouldn't have gotten here.

Jessica Woollard, my brilliant, sassy, super agent who inspires me to read and be so much more, kept us strong, even when we withered. The young cricket guru, Imran Ahmad Khan, whom I met on Sixth Avenue on a cold night on the eve of the Trump election while on assignment in New York, propelled Lala and me to go further.

I must thank Lt Gen. Asim S. Bajwa, my friend and mentor, for connecting me to Lala on a helicopter ride to Khyber.

As for the one and only Amean J, the super hot cover and poster in this book couldn't be imagined without his deep lens.

And without the patience of HarperCollins India's Udayan Mitra and Arcopol Chaudhuri, I'd still be copy-editing voice overs.

Thank you, all. You guys are the best.

ABOUT THE AUTHORS

SHAHID AFRIDI is a former captain of the Pakistan national cricket team. An all-rounder, Afridi was a right-handed leg spinner and a right-handed batsman. He retired from international cricket in 2017. Afridi established the Shahid Afridi Foundation, which aims to provide healthcare and education facilities in Pakistan, in 2014.

WAJAHAT S. KHAN produces and corresponds from Pakistan for *Vice News*, *The Times* and *India Today*. He has reported from fifteen countries covering conflict, diplomacy, politics and media for digital, cable and networks. Before serving as NBC's last bureau chief in Kabul, Afghanistan, Khan also launched Pakistan's first independent Urdu and English cable networks and produced the first broadcast series from across the border in India. He is a 2011 Harvard Shorenstein Fellow, a 2012 Asia Society Young Global Leader, and landed Pakistan's only Emmy nomination for breaking news in 2015, the year he met Shahid Afridi.

Khan last bowled right-arm fast-medium for the Frere House of his Karachi Grammar School with an ageing sniper's accuracy. He can't handle spin, both on and off the field.

30 Years *of*

HarperCollins *Publishers* India

At HarperCollins, we believe in telling the best stories and finding the widest possible readership for our books in every format possible. We started publishing 30 years ago; a great deal has changed since then, but what has remained constant is the passion with which our authors write their books, the love with which readers receive them, and the sheer joy and excitement that we as publishers feel in being a part of the publishing process.

Over the years, we've had the pleasure of publishing some of the finest writing from the subcontinent and around the world, and some of the biggest bestsellers in India's publishing history. Our books and authors have won a phenomenal range of awards, and we ourselves have been named Publisher of the Year the greatest number of times. But nothing has meant more to us than the fact that millions of people have read the books we published, and somewhere, a book of ours might have made a difference.

As we step into our fourth decade, we go back to that one word – a word which has been a driving force for us all these years.

Read.

Harper Collins   HARPER PERENNIAL   HARPER BUSINESS   HARPER BLACK   हार्पर हिन्दी

HarperCollins *Children's Books*   HARPER DESIGN   HARPER VANTAGE   Harper Sport